ROBERT TOLF'S
Destination Florida

Orlando's
International
Drive

Other books by Robert Tolf
in the *Destination Florida* series

Sanibel & Captiva Islands
South Beach, Miami

ROBERT TOLF'S
Destination Florida

ORLANDO'S INTERNATIONAL DRIVE

TRIBUNE
PUBLISHING
Orlando / 1993

Copyright © 1993
Tribune Publishing
75 East Amelia Street
Orlando, Florida 32801

Series Editor: Dixie Kasper
Editor: Deborah Kane Mitchell
Text and jacket designer:
    Joy Dickinson
Text illustrations
    by Franklin Ayers
Cover illustration
    by Larry Moore

TRIBUNE PUBLISHING

Editorial Director:
    George C. Biggers III
Managing Editor: Dixie Kasper
Senior Editor: Kathleen M. Kiely
Production Manager: Ken Paskman
Designers: Bill Henderson,
    Eileen M. Schechner,
    Joy Dickinson

For information:
Tribune Publishing
P.O. Box 1100
Orlando, Florida 32802

Printed in the United States

FIRST EDITION

Library of Congress Cataloging-in-Publication Data

Tolf, Robert W.
    Orlando's International Drive. — 1st ed.
    p.   cm. — (Robert Tolf's Destination Florida)
    Includes index.
    ISBN 1-56943-002-0
    1. Orlando (Fla.) — Guidebooks.   2. International
Drive (Orlando, Fla.) — Guidebooks.   I. Title.
II. Series: Tolf, Robert W.   Destination Florida.
F319.07T65   1993
917.59'24—dc20   93-21127
                                                          CIP

Contents

How to Use This Guide

DESTINATION FLORIDA GUIDEBOOKS ARE WRITTEN for discriminating, eager-to-learn, knowledge-able travelers — first-timers or repeats, one-day trippers, weekend warriors or extend-ed escapees — all those who want to discover or rediscover what Florida has to offer. And it's a lot!

This book is organized into sections dealing with the basics, the where-to-eat and where-to-stay and what-to-see recommendations — only the best — along with practical infor-mation on shopping, souvenir hunting and the necessities — where to find a dry cleaner, photo shop, barber or hairdresser, limo or taxi.

Beyond the logistics of International Drive as support base for all that's going on in Greater Orlando, there's the Bargain Boule-vard aspect of discount shopping and the fun-in-the-sun appeal of miniature golf, Wet 'n Wild, Sea World and Universal Studios.

Bookstores, newsstands and libraries are listed, as are business services for those who want to keep their offices posted while vacationing. Museums are listed for those who want to learn about the culture and history of the area, art galleries for inside strolling and nature trails for outside treks. Those looking for a little night music will find separate listings of lounges with live entertainment, nightclubs, movies, concert halls and theaters.

We have not listed large supermarket and hardware store chains because, if you need their services, they are easy to find when you reach your destination.

The specific prices of accommodations and restaurants are not listed, but we have established the following general cost categories for double-occupancy rooms, and dinner for one including appetizer, main course, dessert and beverage, but not including tax, tip or drinks.

INEXPENSIVE   Less than $15 for dinner for one. Less than $50 for a double-occupancy room.

MODERATE $15 to $30 for dinner for one. $50 to $125 for a double-occupancy room.

EXPENSIVE   More than $30 for dinner for one. More than $125 for a double-occupancy room.

Many restaurants offer savings for the diners who like to eat early, the so-called early birds, and almost all of the accommodations offer seasonal savings from May through December, except in North Florida where the off-season runs from Labor Day to Memorial Day. There are also a great variety of package deals at these accommodations, with terrific savings and all kinds of extras, so be sure to inquire when you call for reservations.

No complimentary lodging, meals, or other considerations and freebies were received in the research and gathering of information for this book.

Tourist Information

Greater Orlando Chamber of Commerce, 75 East Ivanhoe Boulevard, Orlando, Florida 32819. (407) 425-1234.

Orlando/Orange County Convention & Visitors Bureau, Inc., 7208 Sand Lake Road, Suite 300, Orlando, Florida 32819-5273. (407) 363-5800, Convention Services Department: (407) 363-5896.

1220 AM Radio, Tourists Tips, Orlando.

Visitor Information Center at Mercado, Mercado Mediterranean Village, 8445 International Drive, Orlando, Florida 32819. (407) 363-5871.

How to Get Here

International Drive is easy to reach from
Interstate 4, following the clearly marked
signs. Exit 30A takes you to the northernmost
end of Kirkman Road and leads to the Drive a
few minutes away. Exit 29 leads to Sand Lake
Road (State Road 482), which intersects the
Drive. Both exit 27A (the Central Florida
Parkway) and exit 27 (State Road 535), lead
into the Drive close to the exits.

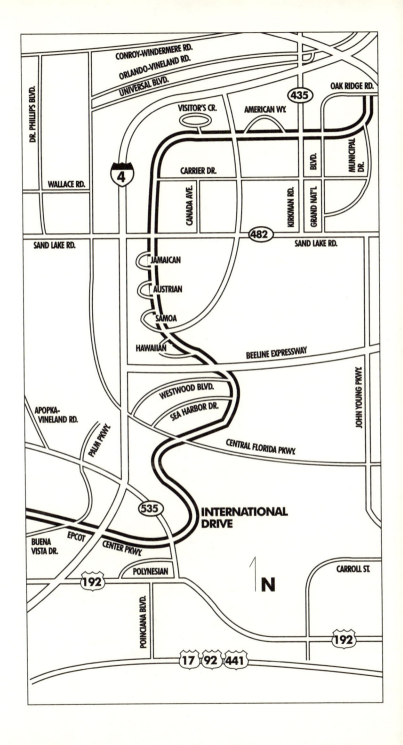

Orlando's
International
Drive

International Drive: Main Street, U.S.A.

That's right, Main Street. Forget all that Magic Kingdom hype about a single block with false facades masking offices upstairs and all that mouse merchandise below.

International Drive is the real Main Street. It's far, far more typical, more representative of fried food freeways across the land, with flashing and clashing nonstop signs screaming for space, traffic that never ceases and hawkers who never stop selling.

International Drive is the real Main Street, U.S.A.

Stand on the corner of International Drive and Sand Lake Road and look north. You'll see Everytown, U.S.A., complete with a gas station on the corner, golden arches and hotels and motels of every size and description. There are general-issue strip malls and enough T-shirt sellers to clothe the Chinese Army. There are snack shops and buffeterias, pizzerias, cafes and restaurants everywhere.

I-Drive bashers see a cacophonous chaos, a driver's nightmare, a street of lost souls condemned to "finding heaven in chain-food hell." A major guidebook dismisses it as a "honky-tonk strip," while another, when listing budget accommodations on the strip, recommends hotels in Tampa, Tarpon Springs and Daytona Beach!

I hear America Singing — updating poet Walt Whitman by a century or so — in these real representatives of life in the United States. This is the kind of life millions of tourists who travel the Drive come to see and to participate in — the modern motel rooms and hidden courtyards of escape Edens landscaped so lushly, complete with swimming pools seldom seen in Europe and beyond. It's a comfort-zone base camp in the heart of the greatest concentration of amusements in the history of the world.

International Drive is where the world meets.

International Drive is where the world meets — to sleep, to eat, to amuse themselves, to dream about having such abundance, such orderly and organized entertainment. They stroll the streets and drive to the shops of one of the discount capitals of the world. They find on the racks the daily papers from back home, in addition to copies of the *Union Jack,* the *Irish-American, Latino Internacional,* and *Treffpunkt Orlando,* Florida's "Aktuelle Deutschsprachige Zeitung," up-to-date German newspaper.

International Drive is not a Boulevard of Broken Dreams, but of good old free enterprise, right down to all those people manning all those "Discount Tickets Sold Here" booths or selling rides on the "mini-est" simulated space ride, wedged into a few feet of free space in front of a fast food restaurant.

International Drive is a monument to American marketing.

International Drive is the capital of chain-food America, the essence of high-volume family chain-feeders. All the giants are here, including the country's first Olive Garden and China Coast. But also on this street of great eats is the best Japanese restaurant in the country and the best Lebanese and best-dressed Indian restaurants in the state.

International Drive is a 10½-mile monument to American marketing and merchandising, anchored by Sea World on one flank and Universal Studios on the other, with lots of room to grow. New hotels and restaurants are popping up, and land is being cleared for other attractions, including a few on streets integral to the Drive and included in our coverage — Republic Drive, Kirkman Road, Dr. Phillips and Major boulevards.

International Drive happened overnight — and it's still looking forward to its silver anniversary.

Only in America.

ACCOMMODATIONS

APARTMENT LOCATOR SPECIALISTS, INC.

APARTMENTS/
HOMES/ CONDOS

7208 Sand Lake
Road, Suite 204
Orlando 32819
(407) 345-1000

Tourists who can't tear themselves away from all the wonders of International Drive and want to settle in for a housekeeping spell should check with these specialists for something more than one of the seemingly innumerable hotel rooms.

BEST WESTERN PLAZA INTERNATIONAL

HOTEL

MODERATE TO
EXPENSIVE

8738
International
Drive
Orlando 32819
(407) 345-8195
Toll-free:
1-800-654-
7160

This Best Western biggie has something for every kind of family need. There are 474 rooms with double beds; 66 efficiencies with double beds and fully furnished kitchenettes; 66 two-room suites with a king-size bed in one room and a double bed and kitchenette in the other; 39 two-room suites with a king-size bed in one room and a living room with sofa bed and kitchen unit in the other. There are also two dozen king-size bedrooms complete with Jacuzzis. On the first floor are rooms specially equipped for the handicapped. There's a large heated pool, a smaller, shallower one for the kids and an outdoor Jacuzzi, along with a poolside snack bar and a Friendly's restaurant, part of a family-oriented chain that is open for three meals a day.

HOTEL

MODERATE TO
EXPENSIVE

*9700
International
Drive
Orlando 32819
(407) 352-9700
(407) 354-1703
Toll-free: 1-800-
627-8258*

CLARION PLAZA HOTEL

A spacious spread with a majestic marble lobby that could accommodate a battalion or two, with a grand piano, neatly planted dividers, bold pillars and handsomely outfitted corners for getting away from it all. The location is perfect for conventioneers, who have to walk only a few hundred feet from the Convention Center to the comforts of the Clarion. Minutes after finishing an exhausting day in or out of the display booths, selling, buying or just looking and learning, the conventioneers can be stretched out on a chaise lounge soaking up the sun, splashing around in the huge free-form pool hedged with a variety of palm trees (tall and taller); taking in the bubbles in the invigorating Jacuzzi, or just returning to the comforts of a spacious, well-appointed room — nothing fancy, but with in-room safes and such necessities as individual temperature control and remote-control TV. There are 778 guest rooms with two queen-size beds and 32 suites, including two-bedroom parlors and presidential suites.

The food service is nonstop, with a 24-hour Lite Bite snack shop, a larger coffee shop called Cafe Matisse and decorated accordingly, and the signature room of the hotel, Jack's Place. Jack is short for Jack Rosen, father of Clarion owner Harris Rosen and a first-generation

American born in New York's East Side of just-off-the-boat Russian immigrants. An artist and engineer, he was employed at the Waldorf-Astoria, and during his three decades there sketched caricatures of some 100,000 subjects, many of them the notables who were at the Waldorf. A small portion of that number have been collected by hotel-owner Harris and now brighten the walls of the restaurant, an intimate affair with paneled walls and a super-solicitous staff (see page 68). The hottest nightclub on International Drive is also on the property, The Backstage Lounge (see page 120).

COMFORT INN INTERNATIONAL

HOTEL

MODERATE

For the water-lovers in the group, this is the perfect location on International Drive — across from Wet 'n Wild. And there's a heated pool, kiddie pool and a pair of shuffleboard courts on the premises. There's also a Denny's on the site, open 24 hours a day. The 162 rooms are functionally attractive, and the architectural design of the two-story units with their barrel tile roofs and fake balconies screening the air-conditioning boxes, is outstanding in a Mediterranean revival kind of way.

5825 International Drive (American Way)
Orlando 32819
(407) 351-4100
Toll-free: 1-800-327-1366

HOTEL

INEXPENSIVE TO
MODERATE

*8600 Austrian
Court off
International
Drive*
Orlando 32819
(407) 351-2244
*Toll-free: 1-800-
321-2211*

COURTYARD MARRIOTT

Here is the Marriott corporate giant writ small, a 151-room hotel tucked into the cul-de-sac end of Austrian Court, adjacent to the Aquatic Center and across the Drive from Mercado Mediterranean Village. There are swimming pools and whirlpools, an exercise room and the usual amenities, including guest laundry facilities.

HOTEL

INEXPENSIVE TO
MODERATE

*5715 Major
Boulevard*
Orlando 32819
(407) 351-3340
*Toll-free: 1-800-
877-1133*

DELTA ORLANDO RESORT

One of only two U.S. Delta links (the other is in Florida's Key Largo) of the Canadian hotel corporation, with 800 guest rooms and suites rambling over 25 landscaped acres dotted with a trio of swimming pools, saunas, a hot tub, sand-base volleyball courts, lighted tennis courts, a children's playground and supervised programs plus a video game room. The three- and four-story units provide a comforting sense of low-rise retreat and are conveniently close to the main gate of Universal Studios. The Center Court Cafe has budget-pleasing breakfast buffets, lunch and dinner specials, and an ice cream parlor that's open until midnight. Mango's has reasonably priced meals three times daily plus live entertainment, and there's more of that at the Waters Edge Bar & Grill with reggae and contemporary pop. Home-style family barbecue is served at the grill Sunday and Wednesday — fun for the kids and food enough for the next day.

THE ENCLAVE

Quietly situated a few hundred meters from the Drive, this trio of Aztec temple high-rises offers 326 studio units and two-bedroom, two-bath suites, each with private patio or balcony and fully furnished kitchenette. The studio has a Murphy bed. The furnishings are light and tropical without frills or finery. With a pair of outdoor swimming pools and one indoors, a lighted tennis court, an exercise area with sauna, steam and whirlpool baths, and a wooden deck playground, this is a popular stopover for groups on package rates — the studio suites can accommodate four guests, the others a total of six, at no extra cost.

RESORT

MODERATE

6165 Carrier Drive off International Drive
Orlando 32819
(407) 351-1155
Toll-free: 1-800-457-0077

THE FLORIDIAN

Another budget-pleasing place, this one with 283 rooms and 17 suites, is located behind Wet 'n Wild. All rooms have VCRs and double standard or king-size beds. The suites have wet bars and refrigerators. Neither the design nor the furnishings are ambitious — but then, neither are the prices. And they offer all the services of more costly digs — self-service laundry, same-day valet service, business support with fax and copying facilities and a guest services desk to answer the inevitable questions and make the arrangements. There's a poolside bar for lunching, snacking and sipping, a lounge and The Palms Cafe and Grill Restaurant, which is open for breakfast and dinner.

HOTEL

INEXPENSIVE TO MODERATE

7299 Republic Drive
Orlando 32819
(407) 351-5009
Toll-free: 1-800-445-7299

HOTEL

INEXPENSIVE TO MODERATE

6233 International Drive

Orlando 32819

(407) 351-3900

Toll-free: 1-800-327-2114

GOLDEN TULIP LAS PALMAS HOTEL

Here's a 261-room money-saver located directly across from all the splashing at Wet 'n Wild. The rooms have been renovated recently, and there's a swimming pool and a playground out back. There's also a money-saving restaurant on the premises, Fiestas. But there are other budget-stretching places to eat all up and down the Drive.

HOTEL

MODERATE

6435 Westwood Boulevard

Orlando 32819

(407) 351-6600

Toll-free: 1-800-527-1133

HAWTHORN SUITES HOTEL

The appeal of this 345-unit all-suite hotel, only a block from Sea World, is what they offer in their one-bedroom, one-bath, and two-bedroom, two-bath accommodations. Each has a fully equipped kitchen, comfortable sitting and dining room with furnishings more functional than fancy. We like such extras as the videocassette players with movie and Nintendo rentals in the lobby, the AM/FM stereo cassette players and the convertible double sofa beds. Outside are the pools for adults and children with an adjacent enclosed playground and a specialty poolside bar offering drinks, sandwiches, subs and pizza. In the exercise room, you can stretch your stressed-out muscles from all that theme park walking and follow it with a session in the whirlpool. Don't worry about where to eat breakfast the next morning — it's included in the cost of the suite.

HERITAGE INN-ORLANDO

HOTEL

INEXPENSIVE TO
MODERATE

*9861
International
Drive*
Orlando 32819
(407) 352-0008

The Heritage Inn is old Florida, complete with a pseudo-plantation facade, rotunda double decks and a wraparound porch graced by comfortable rockers for just sittin' and rockin', whiling away the time, doing nothing and thinking great thoughts about all you've done in just a few days on the Drive. About a minute away is the Convention Center, and next door is the penultimate Peabody. The 150 guest rooms have paddle fans, refrigerators and attractive French doors; and the staff strives to live up to the spirit of the period reflecting slower, more genteel times. The atrium lobby is as unique in this area as the shape of the building. It's the home of The Florida Murder Mystery Players, who put on an audience participation whodunit during your dinner. It's also the setting for live jazz and blues with the 7 p.m. show including dinner in the price of admission — cocktails and a light menu are available for the 9:30 p.m. show. No other hotel has that kind of fun and games in its lobby.

RESORT

EXPENSIVE

*6515
International
Drive
Orlando 32819
(407) 351-5757
Toll-free: 1-800-
HOLIDAY*

HOLIDAY INN
INTERNATIONAL DRIVE RESORT

Sporting one of the most elaborate — and busiest — lobbies of any Holiday Inn in the world, this 654-room model of modern motel management typifies what is magical about so many accommodations on International Drive. It really is a world apart, a place with fun, getaway restaurants, newly refurbished accommodations with twin beds and all the conveniences — and a grand sense of style in the eight executive suites. Accommodations flank the courtyard in two-story units or are in the 12-story tower. But the most magic comes when you go past the Coral Key Bar & Grille with its raw bar and seafood specialties and walk into the courtyard. It's Eden — with a free-form heated pool and rocky waterfall framed by luxuriant landscaping that is constantly being maintained and renewed. Close at hand is a poolside gazebo bar and live entertainment — island music of course. The escape is total, whether you're fleeing the theme parks, the city, bosses, home or all that awful weather.

In addition to the Coral Key restaurant, there's the Front Street Cafe, named for a main drag in Key West and designed with a Key West theme. It's a class coffee shop with a bountiful breakfast buffet, noontime salads, sandwiches and evening seafood buffets. Then there's Gomba Joe's Italian Eatery with its great submarines layered into fresh-baked breads and sold for takeout along with such other tempters as muffins and pastries. There's pasta and pizza galore, and a staff that conveys a great sense of fun in pleasing the guests. Gumbalicious!

For the juniors in the family, there are restaurant visits by various cartoon characters, and an active program of pool parties with hula hoop and limbo contests, volleyball competition and nature walks.

HOWARD JOHNSON

HOTEL

MODERATE

Of the 82 Howard Johnson Hotels and HOJO Inns in Florida (600 in North America), three are on International Drive. They include the 21-story, 303-room landmark with a round tower located at 5905 International Drive. It's had many mortgage-holders over the years and now sports a restaurant and lounge with entertainment and a gift shop. A two-story low-rise spread is at 8020 International Drive, with 150 rooms, a restaurant open for breakfast only, and small swimming and kiddie pools. And there's a 176-room complex of three-story units that also has swimming pools and a restaurant. The tower is across from Wet 'n Wild and is impossible to miss from Interstate 4 or the Florida Turnpike; the 150-room junior of the bunch is at the intersection of International Drive and Sand Lake Road, which leads directly to Orlando International Airport. All accommodations have the usual

6603 International Drive
Orlando 32819
(407) 351-2900
Toll-free: 1-800-722-2900

5905 International Drive
Orlando 32819
(407) 351-2100
Toll-free: 1-800-327-1366

8020 International Drive
Orlando 32819
(407) 351-1730
Toll-free: 1-800-654-2000

Howard Johnson furnishings and spaciousness and provide alternative accommodations to those with deeper wallets. Contact the hotel of your choice at the individual telephone numbers or using the general number of this nationwide chain, 1-800-I-GO-HOJO.

HOTEL

MODERATE TO EXPENSIVE

8001 International Drive
Orlando 32819
(407) 351-2420
Toll-free: 1-800-421-8001

ORLANDO MARRIOTT INTERNATIONAL DRIVE

This is the biggest hotel on International Drive — not in height but in the number of rooms — 1,076 of them — including one- and two-bedroom suites, 77 of them with fully furnished kitchens. The units are spread in unobtrusive low-rises in 16 buildings occupying more than 48 acres. Completely restored and refurbished in 1990, the rooms are up to Marriott standards, and they have the usual amenities. Outside are three swimming pools, two of them with adjacent kiddie pools and one with a whirlpool. In addition, there's a quartet of lighted tennis courts, a playground, a health club, wonderful paths for strolling amid lighted ponds and little lagoons with fountains.

And when you're hit by a case of the hungries, not to worry! This campus has no fewer than seven restaurants and lounges, including two, not one, miniaturized Pizza

Huts on the premises, open 24 hours and delivering directly to your room. The Grove Steakhouse lives up to its name, offering Maine Lobster and seafood in addition to all that beef; the Chelsea Cafe has breakfast and luncheon buffets. When I last stayed here Chelsea had Tuesday and Thursday Lobstermania nights with special dinners built around that red armored knight of the table.

The Crocodilly and Whoppadilly poolside bars sell sandwiches, snacks and tropical drinks. There's also a lobby bar near the gift shop, and the Illusions Lounge with a dance floor and a program of special activities. If you're coming with a group, don't worry about cramped meeting space — there's 27,000 square feet of it and several breakout rooms. You can get your hair done between meetings or fax your messages, have copies made, do your laundry, arrange for baby sitters, and even get language assistance — just check with the guest services desk.

HOTEL

MODERATE TO
EXPENSIVE

*6300 Parc
Corniche Drive
at south
International
Drive*

Orlando, 32821

(407) 239-7100

*Toll-free: 1-800-
446-2721*

PARC CORNICHE CONDOMINIUM SUITE HOTEL

This 260-unit all-suite hotel, located at the southern end of International Drive, is great for golfers who only have to walk a few hundred yards to get to the clubhouse of the International Golf Club (see page 118). Opened in 1990 with three units screened by carefully tended landscaping, the hotel has been successful enough to be building two more units. The one- and two-bedroom guest rooms are spacious with private balconies or patios, couches for lounging, dining tables and fully equipped kitchens. There's a restaurant in the complex, Michael's Cafe, serving complimentary continental breakfasts, lunches built around sandwiches and salads — the Hunter Salad with its heart of palm and pulled pheasant in a fresh tortilla shell is our favorite — and dinners that get as ambitious as pasta primavera, veal Francese or Marsala, chicken scarpariello and filet mignon. There's a heated swimming pool and one for the kids, as well as a whirlpool.

PEABODY ORLANDO

HOTEL

EXPENSIVE

9801 International Drive

Orlando 32819

(407) 352-4000

Toll-free: 1-800-PEA-BODY

1-800-323-7500

This subtropical spinoff from its famous parent in Memphis (regarded since the 1930s as the "South's Grand Hotel") is the grand glory of International Drive. The main tower rises 27 stories and is flanked by two symmetrical stacks that stand as solid sentinels overlooking the gigantic Orlando/Orange County Convention Center across the Drive. You can't miss it. Look for the dandy little duck emblazoned on the pinnacles.

The Peabody is the southern center for the most famous duck act since Donald and Daffy. No mallards ever gained greater fame or had a more sophisticated place to call home. The little duckies, a drake and his harem of four, arrive by elevator at 11 a.m. sharp every morning in the hotel lobby, where they waddle down 70 feet of red carpet to their home away from home, the center court lobby fountain. Tea is served in the ducks' lobby from 3 p.m to 4:30 p.m. with finger sandwiches and petit fours — but please DO NOT FEED THE DUCKS! At 5 p.m, the ducks leave their watery home after a day of splashing and swimming, nibbling and resting, and return to the Royal Duck Palace, located on the fourth-level recreation deck. At their head is the specially appointed duck master. Trained in mallard nutrition and breeding in conjunction with Save the Wildlife, Inc.,

(STW), the duck master has intense hands-on experience, learning, in the words of STW, "the physiological incentives of positive reinforcement within duck behavior, and the importance of the pecking order in training and motivation."

That won't be your concern as you watch the parade or enjoy the ducks during their daylong play in the fountain. Next, treat yourself to one of the special meals in the signature restaurant called, oddly enough, Dux and filled with various designs depicting, you guessed it, ducks, ducks, ducks (see page 60). Mallards Lounge next to Dux also exploits the theme shamelessly and included in the gift shop's inventory of souvenirs, gifts, sundries and casual wear are all kinds of ducks in every conceivable artistic medium.

Those eating opportunities are reason enough to check into this hotel, but there are others we have found during our visits. There's the always-smiling, always-helpful staff, eager to satisfy their guests and professionally supervised to guarantee a high level of performance. Then there's the basic level of comfort, and such conveniences for large groups that may or may not be attending a function across the Drive. There are 54,000 square feet of banquet and meeting rooms. For those guests who want to indulge in a little, or rather a lot, of pampering there's the

privately accessed top three concierge level
floors connected by grand staircases. Afternoon
refreshment and continental breakfasts are
complimentary.

Peach is the basic color in most of the guest
accommodations — 891 of them, including
57 single and bi-level presidential suites
complete with pantries, private balconies and
wet bars. All rooms receive complimentary
newspapers, have mini-bars, TVs concealed
in handsome chests of drawers, a desk and
comfortable sitting chairs plus extra tables for
working or holding the deliveries from the
24-hour room service. Beds, with double
sheeting and comfortable mattresses, are king-
or queen-size. The bathrooms are not only
spacious and extremely well-lighted (too well-
lighted if you're recovering too early from the
night before), but also have thick, thirsty
towels, and a top-quality array of lotions and
shampoos, with a hair dryer and, maybe the
ultimate luxury, a mini TV on the counter.
There's a duck intaglio on the bars of soap
and the Do Not Disturb sign sports a duck
head.

The last time I luxuriated with the ducks,
I spent more time looking out the window
than I did watching TV, but then my room
faced the Convention Center, and in the distance, Walt Disney World's Epcot Center with
its nightly fireworks. Closer at hand is the

sensational swimming pool, a double Olympic heated giant with three lanes roped off for those who want to do more than splash around. There's also a children's pool and whirlpool on the same level, ingeniously built into the fourth story level above the imposing porte cochere with its cascading waterfalls. On the same deck are four lighted tennis courts with pro shop, and the Athletic Club equipped with 15 Nautilus stations, exercise bicycles, indoor whirlpool and sauna, massage and facial studios and lockers. They also offer regularly scheduled aerobics classes.

There's a hair salon, a video game center and a children's hotel for ages 3 through 12 — reservations 24 hours in advance. Parents booked at Dux can park their kids free.

A final plus is the fully staffed business center with facilities for telefax, photocopying, typing, shipping packages and computer rental.

RAMADA HOTEL RESORT FLORIDA CENTER

RESORT

MODERATE

*7400
International
Drive*

Orlando 32819

(407) 351-4600

*Toll-free in
Florida: 1-800-
327-1363*

*Toll-free outside
Florida: 1-800-
228-2828*

Hilton originally opened this property —
when it was one of the few hotels on the
Drive — but Ramada took over and did a
general expansion and rehab. In addition to
the indoor-outdoor swimming pools, there
are shuffleboard and tennis courts, a Nautilus-
equipped exercise room, a playground for the
kids and hair salons for their parents, plus
Captain Brandy's Lounge in the covered
garden. They serve complimentary popcorn
and have a late-night salad and sandwich bar
where you build your own every night from
10 p.m. to 1 a.m. — kind of like the midnight
buffets on the cruise ships. The Roundtree
Restaurant is literally built around a tree. The
396 rooms and suites are attractively furnished
and face the pool courtyard, affording a quiet
retreat from the heart of International Drive
out front, just north of Sand Lake Road.

RESORT

MODERATE TO
EXPENSIVE

*10100
International
Drive*

Orlando 32819

(407) 352-1100

*Toll-free: 1-800-
325-3535*

SHERATON WORLD RESORT

There are close to 500 Sheraton resorts,
inns and hotels worldwide, but few could
be running the kind of occupancy rates this
giant — 28 acres, 788 rooms and suites —
enjoys almost year-round. Its lobby represents
the volume and the evils of functionalism. The
high-ceilinged rectangular box resembles a
railroad station, a modern one without any of
the architectural features of something historic.
And the lobby always seems to overflow with
large and small groups, a cross section of the
world's travelers who put Orlando on their
must-see itineraries.

But a lobby does not a hotel make. For this
resort, it's the acreage and sense of space —
and the proximity to Sea World at the southern end of International Drive. Once you exit
the lobby and enter the courtyard you're in
paradise, lush with carefully tended ponds,
mini-lagoons, and tropical plants screening
three heated pools plus one for the kids and a
whirlpool. There's a quintet of lighted tennis
courts, a miniature golf course, a playground
for the kids and a fitness center for their parents. It all adds up to an oasis. And it satisfies
more than the visual need for getaway
glimpses of all that greenery.

There are poolside gazebo bars offering
every kind of liquid refreshment and snack
stuff, a colorful cart filled with bronzing and
bathing necessities — towels, visors, lotions,
sunglasses and coverups — a Brasserie restaurant and lounge loyal to its name providing a
casual bistro setting with a bit of posh. The
Brasserie Lounge features nightly entertainment, including evenings of sing-alongs,
karaoke where you can be the star, DJs playing the hot hits of the '50s, '60s and '70s,
and a special kind of entertainment, The Elvis
Illusion.

Guest rooms are furnished in tropically
compatible colors — flowered bedspreads and
rattan fan headboards — or in slightly more
formal tones with four-poster beds and
Colonial furniture.

HOTEL

EXPENSIVE

*6677 Sea
Harbor Drive
Orlando 32819
(407) 351-5555
Toll-free: 1-800-
468-3571*

STOUFFER ORLANDO RESORT

The hotel entrances on International Drive
run the gamut of grand design, from
Southern plantation to Colonial, from block-
buster beautiful to drop-dead temple with
waterfalls and fountains. Some are all facade,
masking standard shoebox motels behind all
that Potemkin front. Some, such as the
Stouffer, greet their guests without drama or
excess of design but with the lush landscaping.
At the Stouffer, the drama is inside.

The 10-story atrium has guest rooms neatly
stacked on all sides and is framed by acres of
wonderful green ivy in window-box planters.
There are more plants in the lobby, where the
designers have softened the overwhelming
space by strategically placing islands of
greenery. Those islands flank the marvelous
bi-level lobby piano bar and lounge called
Dolphins. A beautifully sculpted quartet of
dolphins greet guests, who seem fascinated by
water trickling into pools filled with koi — as
real as the birds in a unique cage that is
Victorian in design and Texas in size.

Unique is the key word here. It has to
be applied to the atrium, largest of any hotel
in the world, all 65,000 square feet of it at
the base with a mini-forest of palms and leafy
trees. Hotel shops, services and restaurants
are tucked into ground floor retreats here and
there. Chief among these are the top-flight

restaurants, Atlantis (see page 29), and
Haifeng (see page 64). There's also Trade
Winds, open for breakfast, lunch and dinner.
It's a split personality place, where you can
eat in the wide-open spaces of the atrium or
inside. When we lunch here we usually have
one of the Caesar salads sporting grilled
chicken, calamari, tuna, salmon, swordfish
or steak bits.

For less formal fare, you can check into the
gazebo of a deli, open around the clock and
offering a solid selection of snacks, salads,
sandwiches, wine and beer. We like to order
espresso, taking it to one of the tables slightly
hidden by lattice work, and sipping it slowly.
We sit there in a canyon of modern construc-
tion while bubble elevators glide noiselessly
on their endless roundtrips. On Sundays, the
lobby is the setting for a brunch that is a
real eye-popper and stomach-stretcher. You
can walk off the calories with a tour of Sea
World or, if you're a guest, you can sign on
for a few sets at one of the five lighted tennis
courts, or work out in the fitness center
with its Nautilus stations, Stairmasters,
treadmills, Jacuzzi, wet and dry steam rooms,
and facilities for massage. The kids have their
own supervised playground as well as a room
filled with video games. Kids 6 through 12
years old can be checked into the professionally
staffed day care center — leave your child
there while you're having your hair done in
the hotel salon.

Or the whole family can take to the water, splashing and swimming in the giant pool with its Mediterranean design and poolside Palms bar where there's a full range of tropical drinks and snack stuff.

Those who want to conduct a little business in this atrium castle away from home can check into the fully staffed business center with facilities for fax transmittal and computer use, copying, shipping and secretarial services.

Or maybe you just want to return to your room — one of the 778 spacious accommodations, including 62 suites, furnished with attention to the climate and location — all light tropical colors and furnishings. Doors open out to the atrium and there are all the amenities, including what management calls "in-room refreshment centers." Leave a wake-up call and you'll receive coffee and a newspaper. It's complimentary, like the glass of champagne you received upon arrival. Stay in one of the Club floor rooms and you'll have complimentary continental breakfast as well as complimentary hors d'oeuvres in the evening.

TWIN TOWERS HOTEL & CONVENTION CENTER

The 760 guest rooms and suites in these landmark buildings across the road from the main gate of Universal Studios offer panoramic views of the incredible funscape that has risen out of the sand, citrus groves and cattle ranches. You can look out the window and plan your attack on moviedom the next day. Or, after a strenuous day, you can retire to the junior Olympic-size swimming pool, the Jacuzzi, sauna or exercise room, sending the kids off to their own pool and playground. You can continue your attitude adjustment by lounging around the pool or lobby bars, in preparation for dinner in the Palm Court restaurant followed by a spell in the Everglades Lounge with its live entertainment. It's a high-rise escape.

HOTEL
MODERATE

*5780 Major Boulevard
Orlando 32819
(407) 351-1000*

WYNFIELD INN-WESTWOOD

This hotel has found a way to offer less expensive accommodations while preserving a little style. Its New England front entrance and carefully tended landscape screens what is basically a shoebox design. It has 300 simply furnished guest rooms and a few important extras — complimentary fresh fruit, tea and coffee in the lobby, along with a game room for the kids and a swimming pool. It's also near Sea World.

HOTEL
INEXPENSIVE

*6263 Westwood Boulevard
Orlando 32819
(407) 345-8000
Toll-free: 1-800-346-1551*

DINING

Restaurants

ATLANTIS

I suppose it was inevitable that the planners of a luxury hotel so close to Sea World would use the magical name of the lost island of mythology — somewhere west of the Pillars of Hercules. But they probably didn't know that Atlantis would become synonymous with a luxury signature restaurant that brings great distinction to the hotel.

We like to start our retreat into this enclave of tranquillity with an aperitif at the wonderfully designed Central Florida imitation of a London men's club, Winston's, adjacent to Atlantis. The designers could have put something silly there, something more in keeping with the Atlantis legend or the Sea World theme park. We're glad they decided, for whatever reason, to take a more sophisticated route.

At Winston's we have some quiet moments to study and discuss the menu, going over chef de cuisine Fred Nater's latest creations. (Tastes of the sun he calls them.) Such starters include gazpacho spruced up with avocado and

Stouffer Orlando Resort

6677 Sea Harbor Drive, Orlando

(407) 351-5555

Dinner daily

papaya, jumbo sea scallops enlivened with an interesting combination of boursin and raspberries, and baked codfish cakes with shiitake mushrooms, oranges and a bit of basil over spinach linguine.

It's hard to choose from those selections, but it's even harder to pick an entree among such headliners as the Maine lobster with a wild mushroom risotto accompanied by asparagus and a port-tarragon sabayon; the Canadian Atlantic salmon wrapped in rice paper with cucumber-mint relish; a grilled Gulf pompano with cilantro and lime juice, flattered with a little mango relish; or a braised lamb shank, upgraded with English mustard and ratatouille and enlivened with roasted garlic.

What a pleasure it is to face such dilemmas, especially while listening to the harpist strum her lovely melodies and analyzing the pairings of food and wine, selected from an outstanding California cellar.

B-LINE DINER

AMERICAN

INEXPENSIVE

*The Peabody
Orlando Hotel
901
International
Drive, Orlando
(407) 240-0121
Open 24-hours
daily*

From be-bop to bobby soxers and Elvis
Presley and Patti Page on the Wurlitzer, this is
1950s all the way. With acres of chrome,
enough black and white squares to build a
thousand checkerboards, neon racing ribbons
and blocks of glass brick, this is an Art Deco
reflection of the current craze for diners built
around rock 'n' roll.

But it's more; it's what the brilliant food
and beverage types at the Peabody like to call
"a restaurant within a diner." The menu offers
a lot more than Green Rivers and fried bologna
sandwiches. In tune with the times, they
feature The Healthy Diner menu complete
with the vital statistics for calories, fat, proteins
and carbohydrates. The broiled multi-grain
veggie burger on a whole wheat bun with fresh
fruit cocktail will cost you 373 calories and
give you 20 grams of protein, 9 grams
of fat and 57 carbohydrates; vegetable chili
with pinto beans and a crown of onions,
cheddar and sour cream — 177 calories,
8 grams of protein, 4 grams of fat and 27
carbohydrates — and pasta mingled with
veggies, herbs and basil oil 176 calories, 19
grams of protein, 14 grams of fat and 31
carbohydrates. There's also grilled breast of
chicken, fruit plates, falafel sandwiches and a
catch of the day simply prepared — as one of
my favorite choices was the last time I blasted

back to the past. The generous size fillet of
fresh Norwegian salmon was swiftly seared
and then lightly touched with a slightly
smoky barbecue sauce. It was accompanied by
a harvest of zucchini and yellow squash stir-
fried in a little vegetable oil, and some rice
spiked with cinnamon.

I like the fact that I can see the line chefs
at work doing that searing and stir-frying,
whether I sit at the long, long counter —
longest of any diner in Florida — or in one
of the window-hugging booths or center space
tables. And I also like all the extra touches
taken with food to raise it above — way
above — the level of what's usually found on
diner menus. They spike up the New England
clam chowder with shrimp and celery, pepper-
ing it perfectly; they flatter the fingers of
farm-raised catfish with a papaya-tartar sauce,
the grilled pork chops with apple-sage chutney,
and they glaze their roast chicken with maple
and tabasco, serving it with garlic-zapped
mashed potatoes.

But the B-LINE is traditional enough to let
its prime rib speak for itself, presenting it with
natural juices and creamy horseradish sauce,
and keeping such standbys as chicken pot pie,
regular burgers, BLTs, Reubens and hot
pastrami on the menu. And they have one of
those front counter displays of outrageous
sweets — giant cakes and cookies — and an

old-time soda fountain approach to sundaes, sodas and banana splits.

A final strong recommendation — they are open around the clock and they have an express takeout counter.

BENNIGAN'S

Another link in the nationwide chain, this one has carefully placed nuggets of nostalgia, an inviting bar, spiffy staff and a menu that satisfies lots of cravings for lunching, munching and dining. For years our cravings here have centered on the broccoli-cheese balls which are just begging to be dipped in the honey-mustard sauce. But they also have OK barbecue ribs, steaks, grilled swordfish, pasta primavera, 11 different toppings for their burgers and tortillas overflowing with turkey and guacamole. Start with the chicken-tortilla soup or some chili and finish with the dessert aptly called Death by Chocolate.

AMERICAN

MODERATE

6324 International Drive, Orlando (407) 351-4435 Lunch and dinner daily

ITALIAN

EXPENSIVE

*8445
International
Drive, Orlando
(407) 352-3805
Dinner daily*

BERGAMO'S ITALIAN RESTAURANT

What's a nice German restaurateur named
Al Steigerwald doing running an Italian
restaurant, one with a staff that sings the songs
"From Old Napoli, to Broadway, to the Met"?
Why not? He scored such a success with
Charlie's Lobster House next door (see page
46) and his other seafood restaurants, he could
afford to take a flier into another world. He
selected his backroom team with care, made
sure they buy quality produce, meats and
seafood and that they can tell the difference
between cannelloni and cannoli, penne,
parmesan and polenta. Then he put the words
of that greatest gourmand of all composers,
Gioachino Rossini, on his menu: "The stom-
ach is the conductor who leads the great
orchestra of our passions." Rossini was such an
enthusiastic eater that he moved into an apart-
ment upstairs from his favorite restaurant and
married his cook to make sure she wouldn't
leave him — or his kitchen.

When we were last in this handsomely
appointed Mecca of music, listening to the
staff go through their dual performances,
delivering our food along with "O Sole Mio,"
we were seated in a comfortable booth made
private by a panel etched with the line from
Donizetti's opera "Lucia di Lammermoor,"
Chi me fre — nain tal mo-me-to? (Translation:
Who is it that is making me so mad this
moment?) Of course we had to order the filet
mignon Donizetti, a half-pound of the best
Black Angus served with roasted garlic and

covered with a superlative creamy gorgonzola
sauce freckled with black peppercorns. We
also had the veal Pavarotti, a scallopine with
shiitake mushrooms and a creamy tomato
sauce spiked with brandy. We thought about
ordering a veal chop Milanese, prepared in the
classic manner — breaded and pan-fried —
and served with risotto. The best of the
seafood selections is the grand Zuppa di Pesce
harvest from the deep, and of the dozen possi-
bilities in the pasta department, we like the
perciatelli with wild mushrooms, fresh peas,
prosciutto, sun-dried tomatoes tossed with
extra virgin olive oil and enhanced with fresh
rosemary. For those diners who don't want
anything fancy or frivolous with their fare,
there's a bounty of broiler choices, red snapper,
salmon, swordfish and tuna from watery
sources; veal chop, filet mignon and New York
strips from the land side.

For starters here we usually order clams
basilico and bruschetta, toasted crisp Italian
bread layered with roasted tomato and garlic,
mozzarella and a slight sprinkle of sliced black
olives and bits of fresh basil. For side dishes we
order the sauteed spinach or broccoli, or con-
tent ourselves with the excellent entree sides,
the perfectly al dente dishes of spaghetti with a
simple garlic-oil sauce.

A final plus — and it's a big one — is the
wine list with 60 top quality imports from
Italy. But they should have vintages listed for
more than Angelo Gaja's Babarescos from '78
to '88, especially at the price level of the labels.

AMERICAN

INEXPENSIVE

6014 Canadian Court, Orlando (407) 352-2161 Breakfast, lunch and dinner daily

BOB EVANS RESTAURANT & GENERAL STORE

Talk about American! How 'bout some hot-cakes? Country ham with biscuits? Or just plain biscuits with sausage gravy? Baked apples, a slice of mush, a bowl of grits and some sausage patties? And then, later in the day, after all that gets time to settle, you can dig into country-fried steak, roast turkey and dressing with a side of cranberry sauce, or hickory-smoked ribs, pot roast, honey-cured ham, a back-country version of the English shepherd's pie, this one using sausage of course, along with cheese and peppers.

Come on a Tuesday and the special is cat-fish. Come the day before and it's chicken pot-pie. And on any day of the week there are apple and lemon meringue pies, and some good old-fashioned food. They even have a smokehouse on the premises. They also have an endless stock of country do-dads, dolls, cards, books, fixin's and finery for the kitchen and parlor, sachets and all kinds of miniatures to collect dust. Most everything on the walls in the restaurant behind the general store is for sale — and clearly marked with the price — everything but the skis, snowshoes, a sled and sleigh and farm implements fixed to the walls, and the skillets, spiders and old-time tools displayed over the kitchen.

There are some 260 Bob Evans country restaurants across the nation, but only eight of them have the general store in front — none of the other 28 in Florida are so blessed.

The last two times we breakfasted with Bob, there were handcrafters out front, including a wonderful basket weaver whose stock was hanging all over the great old front porch, a place where Evansites were just a-sittin' and a-rockin' like they were awaiting the arrival of the Wells Fargo.

A final hoop-de-doo for this neat-as-the-proverbial-pin place. There's live entertainment — guitar and a keyboard played by a singing waitress who was born in Budapest — her parents came out in the 1956 Revolution. Now that's American! As American as Bob Evans!

BUTCHER SHOP

AMERICAN

MODERATE

8445 International Drive, #140, Orlando
(407) 363-9727
Dinner daily

The origins of this palace of beef go back to Memphis, Tennessee, and the offshoots are found in Knoxville, Dallas, Chicago — the capital of steak lovers — and Little Rock, Arkansas, where not everyone eats in a McDonald's like our President.

Beef is the headliner here, and it's on glorious red-blooded display in a counter near the entrance. You can select your own slab and grill it yourself, turning and garlic salting under the watchful eye of the chef, who will give you advice on degree of doneness if desired. It's a great gimmick for backyard barbecuers to show off, and for the uninitiated to learn a bit about a recreational activity that has turned into an art form in this country.

This Butcher Shop serves close to half a ton of beef a night during the busiest months, and it's all cut and trimmed on the premises. But it's all Midwestern stock — despite the fact that Florida is second only to Texas in the number of cattle on its ranches. The setting is all dark wood, brass and glass, and the tables are spaced to afford a degree of privacy while you devour the steak, the prime rib and the baked potatoes.

CAFE BRAZIL

BRAZILIAN

INEXPENSIVE TO MODERATE

6540 Carrier Drive, Orlando
(407) 363-7009
Breakfast, lunch and dinner daily

If you're wondering where to find *Bodo de Camarao, Filezinho* and *Feijoada,* look no further. The shrimp sauteed in a light cream sauce made with manioc flour, coconut milk and peanuts; the beef cubes marinated and simmered in red wine, and the rich black bean, pork-smoked meat stew served with collard greens, slices of orange and farofa — the national dish of Brazil — are at the Cafe Brazil on Carrier Drive, just around the corner from International Drive.

The cafe is next door to Brazil Electronics and other Brazilian enterprises. They have a complete menu of what's being served in Sao Paolo and Rio. Everything comes with black beans and white rice — except the spaghetti and ravioli — and those are felicitous plate-mates for the *Bife a Brasileira,* grilled steak topped with fried eggs and served with farofa and French fries, or the *Lombo de Porco a Carioca,* grilled pork medallions presented with homemade Brazilian campanha sauce, or my favorite, the Cafe Brazil — 2001, which translates to a bed of collard greens sauteed with garlic and topped with chunks of chicken, beef, pork and Brazilian sausage covered with slices of banana, egg and orange. *Obrigado!*

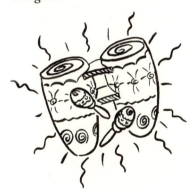

SEAFOOD

INEXPENSIVE

*5648
International
Drive, Orlando
(407) 352-3474
Lunch and
dinner daily*

CALICO JACK'S OYSTER & SEAFOOD RESTAURANT

This local link in a chain of raw bars is fun for snacking late at night or during a midday crisis when you feel the need for a bucket of freshly shucked oysters or clams. Or you could get a burger, steak or the kind of wings made famous in Buffalo when the owner of a restaurant found herself with an oversupply of chicken wings and decided to spike 'em with liquid fire held at bay with blue cheese dressing and celery stalks. Amazing. Only in America.

ITALIAN

MODERATE

*The Peabody
Orlando Hotel
9801
International
Drive, Orlando
(407) 240-0121
Dinner daily
Sunday brunch*

CAPRICCIO

First and foremost is the caliber of the wine list in this delightful trattoria — hands down the best Italian restaurant on International Drive and a lot farther afield. The cellar is extraordinary, the prices unbelievably reasonable, and the breadth and depth unique in Central Florida.

The second reason to be so enthusiastic about this handsomely designed Italian restaurant is the caliber of the professional supervision and the presence of a staff that is friendly, competent and eager to please.

The third reason — and we could make it the first — is the exciting food. There's a regularly revolving cornucopia of the special-

ties of Northern Italy, from a *panzanella* bread
and vegetable salad with cucumbers, sweet
bell peppers, scallions and tomatoes, to *crosti-
ni de fichi,* a spread of sweet figs and virgin
olive oil on parmesan toast; from thin crust
designer pizzas straight from the Tuscan
wood-burning oven to mesquite-grilled
salmon with saffron risotto and red wine
(made from a vintage Amarone!) fish sauce.

We like to start our festive evenings here
with black mission figs wrapped in prosciutto
with a *beurre rouge* sauce — made that way by
the presence of port — or some paper-thin
slices of black angus sirloin carpaccio with
garlic-infused virgin olive oil; and then pro-
ceed to a half-portion of pasta (all eight pasta
dishes come in half and full portions — an
intelligent arrangement), the angel hair tossed
with oil, basil and fresh garlic with some tiger
shrimp or without; or, if I'm waist-watching,
the cholesterol-free whole wheat pasta mingled with vegetables in a light broth.

From there we might finish with the *Pizza
Quattro Stagioni,* the thin-crust flat pie with a
split personality — a quarter each of parmesan,
smoked oysters, mushrooms and prosciutto.
But in such surroundings, and with such
competence in the display kitchen, where you
can see the grill chef working over the flaming
mesquite, we are tempted by the *Bistecca Alla
Griglia,* the grilled tenderloin served with

garlic-parmesan enhanced mashed potatoes; or the pan-seared chunk of yellowfin tuna served on ratatouille, made with sweet bell peppers and served with braised fennel and fried leeks in a saffron-sprinkled aioli sauce.

But we could never eat all that on a Saturday night if we wanted to return the next day for Capriccio's sumptuous Sunday brunch — surely one of the finest in Florida. The eye-pleasing quality of what's spread on the buffet tables would take another page to describe — with equal enthusiasm.

CARUSO'S PALACE

ITALIAN

MODERATE

*8986
International
Drive, Orlando
(407) 363-7110
Dinner daily*

Enrico Caruso died in 1921, but he lives on in this memorial. The 13,500-square-foot, 550-seat pasta pantheon has statues on the roof a la St. Peters in Rome and the cathedral in Milan, with a huge fountain in front and speakers sending operatic arias to the Drive.

It's a re-creation of a 16th-century Italian opera house, and the royal balcony has the great tenor's portrait on it, properly spotlighted of course. It can be seen as soon as one passes under the faux marble pillared arched entry, leading to a giant circular room with statuary and bust-filled alcoves and photos of Caruso's operatic contemporaries.

There are other photos of the Neapolitan and a fine portrait of him, costumed as Pagliacci, by the small bar near the entrance. Center stage is the piano, a digital marvel that sounds like a platoon of musicians. It's built into the fountain and framed by a quartet of Roman pillars. This is where the singers perform, when they're not strolling among the tables, which are built on three levels to allow for maximum viewing of whatever is going on at neighboring tables and in the center court — usually a small group of celebrants having their pictures taken.

The wall and ceiling paintings always make me feel like I'm eating in a baroque church of the late Renaissance, but the chairs and banquettes are far more comfortable than those in any church I've ever experienced. Plush, flowered fabrics for seating complemented by patterned carpeting, and white over raspberry tablecloths provide a comforting sense of formality — you would not want to come here in shorts. The table appointments march right along in creating the ambience of some-thing very Italian, even if it is overblown.

In such a setting, it's not likely the food is going to compete for best Italian on the Drive. And it doesn't, despite the fact that the menu is not a complicated one — a dozen entrees that are as simple as chicken cacciatore, pepper steak, baked salmon with pesto, prime rib, swordfish, and as complicated as veal chop in a roasted red pepper sauce, veal scaloppine in a parmesan-tomato sauce and veal Oscar, prepared in the manner true to its Swedish origins when Caruso was in his 20s and already the toast of Italy — with fresh aspara-gus, lump crab meat and bearnaise sauce.

Included in the price of the entree are the *primo* and *secondo corsos,* soup or salad followed by pasta — my favorite is the *Linguine con Salsiccia,* made with sauteed Italian sausage in a light cream sauce with roasted peppers and various herbs.

The wine list offers sufficient variety and quality to complement the cuisine, and to appreciate more fully the aim of the operators to capture "those qualities of Enrico Caruso's generosity, his love for people of all kinds, his marvelous sense of humor, and his lust for life."

CHARLEY'S STEAK HOUSE & SEAFOOD GRILLE

AMERICAN

EXPENSIVE

*8255
International
Drive, Orlando
(407) 363-0228
Dinner daily*

The person who started this mini-collection of steakhouses — there are several others in the Orlando area — came out of the Red Lobster success. But not all the way when it comes to menu selection — shrimp and catch of the day are available as well as the imports, Alaskan king crab legs and Australian or Caribbean lobster tail. But prime steaks are the order of the night in this comfortably designed restaurant with an upfront grill for guests to see the slabs of beef — and also an occasional chicken and pork chop — being grilled over hard woods.

The menu narrative is a crash course in the Great American Steakmania and guides you to the porterhouse and T-bone, those bedroom slipper-sized steaks that pop the eyes and over-flow the platter. Order them with baked potatoes, some garlic bread — the regular rolls are Parker House style fluff — and dig in. For finishers, what else but a Chocolate Volcano — a mountain of chocolate about to erupt with chocolate fudge swirled with ribbons of white reposing on a rich, moist chocolate brownie. Then celebrate your feast with a final toast, a snifter from their fine cognac collection — Louis XIII if you just won the lottery.

SEAFOOD

INEXPENSIVE TO
MODERATE

*8445
International
Drive, Orlando
(407) 352-6929
Lunch and
dinner daily*

CHARLIE'S LOBSTER HOUSE

The hard-driving dynamo behind this classy seafood server is not Charlie but Al. But he obviously likes the name. His first Charlie's Lobster House and Oyster Bar is in Winter Park; his second in New Smyrna Beach, sitting smack on the Intracoastal Waterway, is called Riverview Charlie's. They all specialize in seafood — fresh Maine lobster, swordfish, red snapper, scrod, dolphin, salmon and Dover sole grilled, broiled, poached, baked, sauteed — whatever. Chef Wendell Thompson in this house can do it all and will honor special requests. Among our favorites are the Coney Island clam chowder, deviled crab cakes, shrimp or scallops scampi and the seafood Newburg. Landlocked palates can retreat to chicken and steaks.

The setting is as special as the quality of the seafood with lots of dark, polished woods and gleaming brass, with intelligent spacing of tables and a fine divider separating the club-by-looking bar. The staff is super-friendly and caring.

For more of the restauranting genius of Charlie cum Al (which is short for Al Steigerwald) go next door to Bergamo's (see page 34).

CHATHAM'S PLACE

CONTINENTAL

EXPENSIVE

*7575 Dr.
Phillips
Boulevard,
Orlando
(407) 345-2992
Dinner daily*

This is a real sleeper of a place for the uninitiated, those who are not residents. It's tucked into an office building across the boulevard from The Marketplace with all its cafes, delis and restaurants so easy to recommend with great enthusiasm.

It's a family operation with the cheffing brothers, Louis and Randolph, working the back room (partially on view) while their mother, Bettye, is in charge of the 75-seat front, furnished in an uncomplicated, Southwestern casual way, a completely smoke-free space. We like that and hope, one day, to find completely non-perfume/cologne spaces in restaurants as well. Then there would be absolutely no interference with the restaurant's nightly appreciation course in the genius of the Chatham boys. They do special things with pasta, and grill the skin of the duck almost to ash, imparting a unique taste while providing fat-conscious diners a good excuse to stop avoiding ducks and order the unique preparation.

Their interpretations of Cajun cuisine are equally original — and blessedly restrained — and we like the manner in which they cook and carve their vegetables, displaying as much pride in the appearance of their offerings as in the tastes and textures. But don't take our word for all the above praise — see and taste for yourself; you'll be experiencing one of the best restaurants in Central Florida.

CHINESE

INEXPENSIVE TO
MODERATE

*7500
International
Drive, Orlando
(407) 351-9776
Lunch and
dinner daily*

CHINA COAST

There are more than 28,000 Chinese restaurants in this country and several food service corporations have tried to cash in on that craze and organize chain operations. General Mills, with more than a thousand of its fabulously successful Red Lobster and Olive Garden restaurants in its portfolio, might be the one to make it work. This one certainly does. It was the first, opened in February 1990, and there are already eight, as far afield as Indianapolis and Dallas-Fort Worth.

With its finely crafted wooden pagoda architecture, bamboo plantings, Asian staff and a general sense of tranquillity and simplicity, this first of the first offers a lot of promise for future growth. We like the made-to-order approach by the kitchen, the presence of a dozen dim sum — such delightful appetite-building starters as pan-seared pot lickers, shrimp, vegetarian and chicken egg rolls, barbecued pork-filled buns, Szechuan wontons and honey-garlic chicken wings. There are complete dinners, called Dragonboat, Emperor and Sampan, consisting of such favorites as orange beef, sweet and sour shrimp and General Tso's chicken. They might change the name to General Mills.

The various offerings are grouped by
Chinese regional cuisine and the back room
handles the spicing well, adjusted according to
the guest's requests except for MSG. They do
not use it. The luncheon buffet is a real budget stretcher for families and is far better than
most such spreads in Chinese restaurants with
less talent or integrity.

Cloning is not going to be a cake wok, but
we think there's a success message in the
General Mills' fortune cookie.

ITALIAN

MODERATE TO
EXPENSIVE

*7600 Dr.
Phillips
Boulevard,
Orlando*

(407) 345-8770

Dinner daily

CHRISTINI'S RISTORANTE ITALIANO

There are so many write-ups — all of them
glowing of course — awards, certificates of
merit and testimonials on display here that
the walls might collapse. They're a main focus
in this elegant enclave with handsome table
appointments, a restrained use of flowers and
greenery with a formally clad staff of waiters
and captains. They're almost as proud of the
place and as promotion-conscious as owner
Chris Christini who, we are informed by one
of the flyers available at the entrance, chose as
an emblem for his restaurant a mini mosaic of
charioteers because they "symbolize his
courage, energy and spirit as he strives to con-
quer the world of fine dining."

That striving has been going on for close to
40 years and has taken Christini from New
York City's 21 Club and The Four Seasons to
hotels in Montreal and Boston and finally
to Central Florida, where he opened Epcot's
L'Originale Alfredo's de Roma, a spinoff of the
famous Roman landmark where Alfredo started
mixing cheese and butter with fettuccine. I've
never had that dish here — or many other
places — because over-enthusiastic waiters
insist on adding cream and too much cheese
converting the conglomerate to wallpaper
paste. But I have had Christini's homemade
pasta in a variety of other forms and flavors,

and I have ordered various chicken and seafood dishes which justify all the high-flowing words of praise on the walls. The filet mignon, a prime cut of beef, and the 26-ounce veal chop are alone worth the trip, made all the more memorable by the strolling musicians — a grand Roman touch — and the roses presented to the women upon leaving.

CRAB HOUSE

SEAFOOD

INEXPENSIVE TO MODERATE

Goodings International Plaza

8291 International Drive, Orlando

(407) 352-6140

Lunch Monday through Friday

Dinner daily

Located a few hundred crab shells north of Mercado, this oversized seafood shack opened in 1993 and is doing, in a high ceiling, cavernous space, what the little guys in real shacks and screened-in outdoor enclosures do with gusto on the shores of the Chesapeake Bay — serving do-it-yourself blue crabs steamed and spiced Maryland style with Old Bay or given the garlic treatment.

You do the picking and the hammering — with wooden mallets. Don't worry about the tablecloths, there aren't any. They use wrapping paper — the real crab shacks use newspapers — for you to make a mess on and for the wait staff to write their names on — well, it's better than "Hi! I'm David and I'm your waiter tonight."

There are more than steamed blues, smiling servers and a large upfront bar with TVs for the die-hards and sports fans. There's a fine salad bar that always seems to be freshly stocked and policed; and there's also a seafood bar with schools of peel-'em-yourself shrimp, shucked oysters and mussels, and of course those crabs. The back room also brews a pretty good gumbo with shrimp, crab and andouille sausage and knows how to prepare crayfish etouffee in the best back bayou manner — someone in the kitchen must be a good ole boy from Louisiana. But they also serve Maine lobster, Florida stone crabs during the October 15 through May 15 season, broiled or grilled swordfish, coconut-coated fried shrimp, prime rib and pasta.

ENGLISH

INEXPENSIVE

Mercado Mediterranean Village
8445 International Drive, #110, Orlando
(407) 354-0686
Breakfast, lunch and dinner daily

THE CRICKETERS ARMS

Only in Orlando! Only on International Drive would there be 400-year-old timbers from Sussex, an etched portrait of legendary cricketer Graham Gooch looking out from a Tudor bar with a gallery of his competitors all around, and authentic artifacts reflecting Britain's national sport. Come in on Saturday mornings and you can argue the point of whether another game doesn't qualify for the title — English soccer is broadcast live. Watch it while having a pint of Guinness, or rather a jug, all 20 ounces of it. Or some Bass Ale,

Harp Lager, or any one of the dozen other
British draft imports on tap. There's also a
stock of bottled beer, plus wine, ports, sherries
and a kitchen that knows how to make a proper puddin' — steak and kidney pudding. Or
fish 'n' chips, Scotch eggs, shepherd's pie and
other good pub grub. Sunday means roast, and
that, too, makes this touch of bonnie Britain
something special.

AMERICAN

INEXPENSIVE

*8445
International
Drive, Orlando
(407) 352-5984
Lunch Monday
through Friday
Dinner daily*

DAMON'S

Among the many International Drive eating discoveries and derivations — which only the ineffably stuffy look down their palates and dismiss as deviations — are those restaurants that keep on ribbin'! Not out-of-the-way joints and ramshackle hideaways, but dressed-up dudes who add a little class to compensate for all the chain chaps who do their ribbin' by the numbers. This place is somewhere in the middle — part of a chain, but with upscale-yet-casual surrounds and a menu that features lean and meaty ribs slathered with their own zesty, not-too-sour, not-too-sweet, not-too-strong barbecue sauce. They also specialize in prime rib, serving it in regular, king and super size, either char-grilled plain or crowned with chopped garlic and butter. But there's also chicken that's barbecued or char-grilled and placed on a bed of rice pilaf, combined with a pair of cheeses and mingled with a harvest of greens, or layered in a toasted poppyseed bun with lettuce and tomato.

But no matter what you order, be sure to get the eye-popping onion loaf and don't worry about the cholesterol count; Damon's uses canola oil. And at the end of the meal add a few more calories and grams of everything by completing your all-American experience with a slice of warm, baked-outback apple pie and vanilla ice cream.

DARBAR

INDIAN

INEXPENSIVE

*The Marketplace
7600 Dr.
Phillips
Boulevard,
Orlando*
(407) 345-8128
Dinner daily

The subdued, sophisticated setting is surely
the most attractive and appealing of any
Indian restaurant in the state, a reflection of
interior design in the days before the Raj,
before the British. The all-encompassing sense
of tranquillity and the good taste provide a
fitting retreat, escaping, if only for a few
hours, all the hustle and bustle of the world.
Sit back and spoon your way through a bowl
of Mulligatawny soup, accompanied by bits of
the special breads, the nam, paratha and
papadum dabbed with one of the chilis and
chutneys before you — remembering to ask
first which are liquid fire and which are only
two-alarm.

After that promising beginning, fill the
table with dishes so you can really appreciate
the talents of the kitchen. Start with a base of
basmati rice and more of the breads along
with beef, lamb or chicken curry, again
remembering to specify the degree of heat,
and some chicken from the high-intensity
heat tandoor (where those breads are swiftly
baked and browned), marveling at the reddish
tones brought out by the marinade. To quell
the flames of anything too hot, remember the
raita, the soothing yogurt with cucumbers or
mint.

If you want to spend a few more rupees,
order the lobster tandoori, and if you want to
save a few, stick with one of the 14 vegetarian
dishes. While your group is making up its

collective mind, nibble on a samosa or two, those freshly fried crescents of dough filled with meats and vegetables, and remember to order Indian beer to calm the curries and salute the occasion.

AMERICAN

INEXPENSIVE

8282 International Drive, Orlando (407) 351-1883 Lunch and dinner daily

DARRYL'S RESTAURANT & BAR

What a fun place! An instant old rambler of brick, brass and wood rusticity that's filled with the outpourings of many an attic and warehouse, office building, gas station, carnival and circus. Tacked up on the walls is every kind of collectible from vintage golf clubs to snowshoes, helmets for football players and helmets for firefighters, weathered advertising signs, an old gas pump or two — remember Skelly? You can sit in an old Ferris wheel car or inside a brass rod elevator cage — they're on the second deck, extended a bit over the bar. I like to sit close to the railing, looking down at the action, wondering who was clever enough to design that lighthouse spiral staircase leading up from the second floor to the ceiling.

The fun continues with the menu, a distinctive tribute to American culinary ingenuity with the Statue of Liberty proclaiming that it's "dedicated to the proposition that all menus are not created equal." Not this one with its armadillo eggs — Cheddar cheese stuffed jalapenos that are lightly breaded, quickly deep-fried, then rushed to the table with a barbecue sauce for dipping. Or Cajun-coated catfish and a dish I seldom can resist ordering, the twice-baked smashed potato with lumps to prove it's the real thing, plus bits of real bacon, a little cheddar, butter, sour cream and scallions, and, for its second trip to the oven, a light layer of Old English Cheese. The menu advises it's "intended for those inclined to dine on the extraordinary."

The soups here are worth considering, ordered separately or in combination with a salad, a quiche (my favorite is the Florentine with mushrooms, onions, Swiss and Cheddar and, of course, spinach) or a turkey BLT. Even better are the meat loaf sandwich grilled on sourdough bread, crowned with Monterey Jack and served with barbecued onions, and the charbroiled Cajun chicken sandwich with the ingredients of a classic Philly — provolone, green peppers and onions. Available at dinner-time for light appetizers are burgers and sandwiches, along with prime rib, T-bone and top sirloin steaks and barbecue pork back ribs.

AMERICAN

INEXPENSIVE

*9880
International
Drive, Orlando
(407) 351-1581
Breakfast, lunch
and dinner daily
Open 24-hours*

*7660
International
Drive, Orlando
(407) 352-9335
(407) 351-1420*

*5825
International
Drive, Orlando
(407) 351-5127*

DENNY'S

Three of the 139 restaurants in the nationwide Denny's fast food chain are located on
International Drive, one close to Sea World
(9880 International Drive), one near the
intersection at Sand Lake Road, (7660
International Drive) and one near the intersection at Kirkman Road (5825 International
Drive). The food is prepared to order by a
chef partially on view through the pass-
through window behind the counter, and the
prices are right for families. For breakfast we
like the All-American Slam with cheese-
infiltrated scrambled eggs, a rasher of bacon
and some pork links along with grits (better
than the home fries that taste like crispified
prefab stuff), toast or muffins. You can also
order a Southern Slam with biscuits and
sausage gravy, or an International Slam with
Belgian waffle and French toast. Later in the
day there are fairly good soups, a lot of fried
stuff, sandwiches and burgers, and other slams
with chicken, ham and prime rib. The
Mother Butler pies are a specialty.

DONATO'S ITALIAN MARKET, PIZZERIA, DELI AND RESTAURANT

ITALIAN

INEXPENSIVE

5159 International Drive, Orlando
(407) 363-5959
Lunch and dinner daily

This really is a four-way treat. The deli counter is near the entrance, serving as a good appetite stimulant as you survey the cheeses, meats, freshly baked breads and wonder whether you want to eat in or go the takeout route. Then there's the market with additional temptations and the pizzeria that has nothing in common with the chains all about. We like the simple little trattoria where we can sit in quiet trying to decide between thin and thick crust pizzas and whether or not to try one of the thickly layered subs. The prices are right. The location is right — close to the Belz Factory Outlet World. And they do deliver.

AMERICAN

**MODERATE TO
EXPENSIVE**

*The Peabody
Orlando Hotel*
*9801
International
Drive, Orlando*
(407) 352-4000
*Lunch and
dinner daily*
Jackets required

DUX

Forget the cute name and be tolerant of all
the ducky drawings and portraits, the butter
forms and handles on the domed silver entree
covers — removed so ceremoniously by the
formal staff. This is, after all, the Peabody,
and the ducks must be given their due. But
they're not on the menu. There's no Peking
duck, no canard Chambord to be found in
this elegantly appointed signature dining
room, one with a fine little European-style
upfront bar and tiny staging area in front of a
fine display of wines.

I like to embark on an evening of sophisticated dining and conversation with the Dux
kind of greeting — a burst of beautifully
arranged flowers, an array of champagne bottles and a formal maitre d' who doesn't tell
any jokes about ducks.

After a bit of bubbly, sipped while survey-
ing and appreciating a setting that is oh-so-
civilized after a day on the Drive or in the
parks, I like to be presented with a menu
reflecting so intelligently the season and performance of local markets and suppliers.
When last indulging at Dux, that bill of fare
was titled "Decisively Dux" and presented
"Food and Wine Pairings that show the culinary Wizardry of Chief Maurer and the
Uniqueness of Dux."

That translated into such seductive stun-
ners as warm Turtle Creek goat cheese,
Belgian endive and watercress laced with fresh
raspberry vinaigrette paired with Edna Valley
Napa chardonnay; coconut milk marinated
sea scallops with mixed baby greens, fried
yucca chips and guava vinaigrette paired with
Jean Claude Chatelaine pouilly fume; and a
Texas veal chop grilled over mesquite with
Zellwood corn custard, wild rice and herb-
cabernet sauce mated with a Sterling
Diamond Mountain Ranch cabernet.

Other menu items — singletons without
inclusive wine — that encourage me to do my
own duck parade to Dux, include roasted
medallions of Atlantic salmon with organic
couscous, pearl onion-raisin confit and a
sweet onion balsamic vinaigrette; and the
Amish roasted chicken, raised not just as a
free-range chicken, but on a 100 percent natural vegetable diet. The bird is glazed with a
combination of coriander and honey and
served with a pear-zinfandel sauce and wild
rice.

Closer to home than the plains of Texas or
the farms of Pennsylvania is the Key West
pompano — our very own Dover sole — that
is lightly seared and served with Island greens,
a mango coulis and a stack of hay made with
sweet potatoes — all good Florida ingredients
as special in flavor as that corn from
Zellwood.

ITALIAN

INEXPENSIVE

*7600 Dr.
Phillips
Boulevard,
Orlando*

(407) 351-1187

*Lunch and
dinner daily*

ENZO'S

The indomitable Enzo, whose restaurant of the same name in Longwood has been a stunning lakeside success for years, opened this trattoria-deli-pizzeria-bakery in June 1992 to meet the needs of modern munchers and diners who want the simplicity of a cafe setting with less fuss and lower cost, and with a kitchen on view. We start our trips here with a survey of the upfront counters, building appetites as we look, readying ourselves for some of the superb vegetable soup with a sprinkle of parmesan and hearty croutons, the carpaccio of filet mignon or one of salmon, thin-sliced Norwegian farm-fed fish marinating in spiced olive oil with lemon, capers and onions on the side.

There's a fine choice of pasta, including our favorite test of an Italian kitchen, the *capelli de angeli,* angel hair with freshly crushed tomato hearts and a touch of basil. Enzo passes the challenge with flying colors, as he does with his homemade spaghetti softened with olive oil and enlivened with fresh basil, Italian pine nuts and parmigiana. There's also American pizza and gourmet Italian pizza. What's the difference? The Italian pies have more pizazz — like toppings of olive oil, mushrooms, fresh garlic, red pepper and parsley; veggies and mozzarella; freshly crushed tomatoes, fontina and mozzarella, chili peppers, green onion and sliced black olives. *Magnifico! Benvenuti* to Enzo's.

FLORIDA BAY GRILL

SEAFOOD

MODERATE

*8560
International
Drive, Orlando*
(407) 352-6655
*Lunch and
dinner daily*

This is a success story of a different stripe on International Drive, one that has a lot to do with a local Burger King king, Manny Garcia, (who is now a major Miami Sub franchisee as well.) From the burger base, Garcia expanded into top-quality cafes, the Pebbles trio in Greater Orlando, and in 1992, into this crisply clean, blue and white bistro with a stellar staff of smiling, eager-to-please professionals.

The menu represents new departures from the seafood serving norm. At noontime you can have a Cajun swordfish sandwich with angel hair onions, char-grilled mahi-mahi with lemon-thyme butter and stir-fried vegetables, blackened rainbow trout with a cucumber-tomato salsa, or a croissant filled with roast beef enlivened with caramelized onions and a few slices of Jarlsberg. Order any of the above with a cup of their excellent conch chowder, a unique presentation that could send Key West cooks back to the drawing boards — it's the color of a rich New England blend, creamy and just spicy enough to make you glad you ordered it.

Among the dinner offerings we favor are the shrimp Alfredo with basil and garlic, the spicy roast duck with pecan-sour orange glaze, the Cajun sea scallops with lemon-splashed pesto, or one of the eight seafood-pasta combinations, the Florida style mixed grill or roasted swordfish with toasted peanuts and lime ginger sauce, and, on the simple side, a New York strip sirloin or a Maine lobster.

But no matter what you order, make sure you have the coconut Key lime pie. In a state where every other chef tries to be creative with Key limes, Florida Bay has the winner. You can salute their success, and the genius of Garcia with a glass of premium wine — 23 of their bottles are available by the glass.

CHINESE

MODERATE TO EXPENSIVE

Stouffer Orlando Resort

6677 Sea Harbor Drive, Orlando

(407) 351-5555

Dinner daily

HAIFENG

Did you wonder about the pair of giant Asian lions guarding the entrance doors of the Stouffer Resort when you first arrived? I did, and was pleased to learn that they were probably there to signal an Asian restaurant inside, somewhere in that massive, overwhelming atrium.

Haifeng is its name and it's hidden behind the multilevel Dolphins lobby bar, tucked into a corner without fanfare or any excess of the kind of red paper lantern/golden dragon designs found in so many Chinese restaurants in the U.S. and abroad.

The decor here is as restrained as the chefs are expansive, cooking the culinary traditions of the mainland — Mandarin, Hunan, Peking, Shanghai and Szechuan along with the much more common Cantonese. For a full-scale, let-it-all-hang-out display of their talents — before your very eyes as the chefs hold court — order the Haifeng Imperial Dinner. You start with a Shanghai-style egg roll containing Chinese vegetables, minced pork and baby shrimp, and move on to honey and sesame-coated deep-fried fish, along with some crab meat Rangoon wontons, followed by a soup featuring dumplings filled with shredded ham and Chinese vegetables suspended in a light chicken broth. Szechuan beef with peppers and scallions in a tangerine hot sauce is the next course along with Shanghai lobster accompanied by broccoli and mushrooms in a snowy sauce made from egg whites. Alongside is some rice fried with pork, minced shrimp and vegetables, and for finishers there are the kind of desserts one associates with top-flight hotels more than neighborhood Chinese mom-and-pop operations.

If you want to avoid that kind of banquet, you can simply order some Hunan lobster — meaning with lots of ginger and some peppers — or a Peking duck prepared in the classic manner. And if you want something else, discuss it with the waiter, or maybe the chef who prepares everything to order. This is a good change-of-pace place, and the service is certainly up to Stouffer standards.

AMERICAN

MODERATE

*5800 Kirkman
Road, Orlando*
(407) 351-7625
*Lunch and
dinner daily*

HARD ROCK CAFE

The first Hard Rock opened in London in
1971, and I was there, wondering why there
was already a line out front; today there are
23 of them from Stockholm and Singapore to
San Juan. It's been wildly successful — and
profitable, owned by a division of Rank
Organization PLC in London but with an
Orlando headquarters. And this $5 million
cafe shaped like an electric guitar with
entrances from outside and inside Universal
Studios, is equally popular, so if you want to
avoid the real crowds come between 11 a.m.
and noon for lunch and 2 p.m. to 4 p.m. for
snacking instead of dining. But no matter
when you work your way in, you'll be dining
in a din. This is not exactly the place to carry
on any kind of conversation, but it is a place
to pay homage to Buddy Holly, Elton John —
his stage costume was the first bit of rock
memento acquired — and of course the King.
You can see up close Bo Diddley's box guitar,
Michael Jackson's shoes, Presley's army
uniform from *G.I. Blues,* plus a bunch of gold
and platinum records of the greats. And
you'll hear their music — oh yes! you will
certainly hear their music — as you work
through the simple menu of burgers and
barbecue, chicken, seafood, salads and
scrumptious desserts, and wait to buy your
own mementos of the visit — the Hard Rock
T-shirt is the most popular in the world.

HOOTERS

AMERICAN

INEXPENSIVE

5300 Kirkman Road, Orlando
(407) 354-5350
Lunch and dinner daily

"Delightfully Tacky, Yet Unrefined," is the way the owners like to describe this local link in the chain that now numbers more than 100. Another of the Florida-born nationwide smashing successes — this one is more exploitative than the others, with the carefully screened waitresses garbed in high-cut camp shorts and low-cut tank tops. The menu is snack stuff, burgers and sandwiches, chicken wings and fresh shuckings from the raw bar.

AMERICAN

MODERATE

Clarion Plaza Hotel

9700 International Drive, Orlando

(407) 352-9700

Dinner daily

JACK'S PLACE

Located off the Clarion Hotel's super-sized marble lobby, this quiet, intimate little paneled dining room is distinguished by the presence on the walls of many of the most famous caricatures by Jack Rosen, father of hotel-owner Harris Rosen. You'll have little trouble picking out Gandhi, former presidents Richard Nixon and Gerald Ford, Sammy Davis Jr., General MacArthur or Nikita Khrushchev, but check out the others — it's a crash course in contemporary history. The sketches show more imagination than the menu, which is basic American hotel fare. Start with shrimp cocktail, smoked Norwegian salmon and oysters on the half-shell served with horseradish, but there's also angel hair pasta marinara sprinkled with grated fontina and cracked black pepper, and a snail-Cajun oyster combo mingled with pasta in roasted red pepper sauce. Among the 14 entrees we like most are the slow-roasted prime rib, the blackened grouper flattered with lime butter, a fillet of salmon on a cedar plank, and the shrimp sauteed with a carefully balanced blend of garlic and other herbs, a dollop of butter and a splash or two or three of chardonnay. The service, starting with the highly professional performance of the maitre d' at the host's podium, is as competent as it is friendly.

JONATHAN'S STEAK & SEAFOOD GROTTO

SEAFOOD

MODERATE

*5600
International
Drive, Orlando
(407) 351-7001
Lunch and
dinner daily*

What's a stone and statue-filled grotto complete with Neptune straddling a waterfall doing on International Drive? Why not? It may look like the third hole of a miniature golf course, but it's really a restaurant. It was built to look that way because a few years ago the West Virginia owner wanted to make his place stand out from the mediocrity of mall architecture. Now he's calling his creation The Lost City, attracting the curious and promising that "Aqueducts, Waterfalls, Japanese Koi, Statues, Carved Rock Work & Lush Foliage Make Every Meal A Dining Adventure!"

That adventure starts with stone crab claws or soft-shell crabs, (when either of those treasures from the deep are available fresh from the supplier), king and snow crab claws flown in frozen from Alaskan waters, lobster from Maine, and fillets of fish from the waters of the world including scrod from Boston and orange roughy from New Zealand. The last time I was in the Lost City I had an excellent slab of blackened salmon and the time before that a shrimp-scallop mating that was bedded down with properly al dente linguine.

Also available are a half-dozen pastas, including something really different, beef tenderloin tips swimming in a marsala sauce tangled with angel hair. Heartier, landlocked appetites have prime rib, steaks and chops for comfort, along with filet mignon that's been subjected to a bleu cheese marinade.

We like to start our adventure with a trip up to the bar-lounge, high in the treetops with a great overview of all the action down below, where there's enough greenery to start a nursery. Then we sit and sup on the lowest level, alongside the trickling waters, wondering what all those fish are thinking about as we fork into another fillet of flounder.

MEXICAN

INEXPENSIVE

*Mercado
Mediterranean
Village
8445
International
Drive, Orlando
(407) 363-0613
Lunch and
dinner daily*

JOSIE O'DAY'S

With the demise in the summer of '93 of the International Drive link in the national Casa Gallardo chain, this attractive ramble of rooms in Mercado now stands alone as the purveyor and provider of Tex-Mex stuff — sizzling fajitas, tacos and tamales, enchiladas and chili rellenos, proceeded of course by a basket of crisp and warm chips with a bowl of salsa. Josie's version is red, but not red-hot. There's no such insult to the palate in this gentled version of a South of the Border cantina.

After all, it is on the corner of DeSoto and Fort Caroline avenues and has to do something other than blow off your sombrero with jalapenos. *Si, senor!* They do lots more, like making all-vegetable fajitas, and serving charbroiled medallions of pork with a field of onions, pico di gallo, rice and refried beans. Then there's the Tex-Mex Skillet, defined as a base of fried potatoes covered with seasoned beef or chicken, topped with spinach sauce and melted cheese, and sent to the table with all the sizzle and smoke of a fajita.

They also do a fantastic grilled chicken salad, a super size serving easily enough for two and consisting of alternate strips of freshly grilled white meat and toasted, crisp tortillas, with lots of red onion rings, real olives, a pico de gallo sweetened with pineapple, and a superb honey-Dijon dressing. If that's not enough for you, order a filet mignon or New York strip steak. They're also excellent, but then this cheerful cantina is owned by the Butcher Shop boys a few doors away and their beef is beautiful.

This is Flo-Mex at its best in a setting with restrained use of the pinata-Zapata approach to South of the Border design. The papier-mache parrots, the brightly colored lizard paintings, and above all, the great wooden, mirrored bar in the lounge remove this from the all-too-common-and-cute kind of decorations found wherever nachos, tostados and burritos are sold. *Muchas gracias,* Josie!

AMERICAN

INEXPENSIVE

*8255
International
Drive, Orlando
(407) 351-6588
Lunch and
dinner daily*

JUNGLE JIM'S

Silliness supreme! Or what the menu promises to be an "Epic Dining Adventure of Lost Legends, Forbidden Pleasures & Ancient Rituals." The adventure is launched with one of the Magical Mindbenders, Tequila Tranquilizers or Electrifry'n Elixirs mixed by Doctor S'Tiph Shotta Likker and his staff of luunee mindfry'd chemists from their collection of Nobel prizewinning Laboratory Libations.

You get the picture? There's more, much more, like Super Sippers for Kids from the Chickabiddy's Choices side of the menu, and Planet Earth's Medley of 63 World Class Burgers. That's right, 63! With every imaginable add-on and combination of ingredients. Number 63 is the World Famous Headhunter and it has a full pound of USDA Choice charbroiled ground beef, grilled ham, a pair of bacon strips, Monterey Jack and Cheddar cheese, lettuce and tomato, dill spears, olives and a pound of their World Famous French Fries. Clean the plate of everything but the napkin and toothpick, and the next one's on the house.

Of course you have to come back and eat among all the animals — not your fellow munchers, lunchers and diners, but all those creatures of the jungle alongside, overhead and underfoot. You can be your very own Jungle Jim.

LA SILA RISTORANTE

ITALIAN

MODERATE TO EXPENSIVE

4898 Kirkman Road, Orlando
(407) 295-8333
Lunch Monday through Friday
Dinner daily

This is more or less Northern Italian cuisine, filtered through the parent operation of the same name in Long Island and defined in such house specialties as fettuccine mingled with smoked salmon in a light cream sauce, penne with arugula and finely diced tomatoes, and that standard tribute to the humble shoemaker, chicken scarpariello with lots of fennel sausage, chopped cloves of fresh garlic, white wine and a hint of vinegar. There's also beef braciola, veal parmesan and a *zuppa di mare* with a boatload of shellfish. We like most the broiled veal chop with the superb sauteed string beans, spinach or rape, softened with olive oil and heightened with garlic. The wine list is OK, and there's a pianist on duty every weekend.

CHINESE

MODERATE

*9188
International
Drive, Orlando*
(407) 351-9988
*Lunch and
Dinner Daily*
*Saturday and
Sunday dim sum
brunch*

MING COURT

What Ran-Getsu (see page 80) represents in
Japanese style, this magnificently ornate,
almost overwhelming, imperial palace shouts
out for the Chinese. Close to 6,000 square
feet of courtyard, terrace, gardens, meeting
and dining rooms are served by a knowledge-
able staff eager to add to the ambitious design
with mu shu pork, dim sum and grilled filet
mignon Szechuan style (made with stir-fried
vegetables zapped with chili oil and cilantro).
It is arguably the ultimate Chinese dining-out
experience, one that is strategically located
only a short walk from the Convention
Center. But you don't have to be in a meeting
to enjoy the fare in this Court. Start with
some of the skewered chicken or a bowl of the
hot and sour South Sea conch chowder, and
then prepare for stir-fried jumbo shrimp
mingled with fresh shitake mushrooms,
tomato, scallions and snow peas, saluted with
ginger and a splash or two of sake. Or indulge
in the roast Peking duck, served in two courses
and not requiring advance notice; or the stunner of a hotpot, brimful with a harvest of
shellfish including lobster and conch swimming in a fine broth brewed with ginger and
garlic, fresh basil, tomato and sake. And if

that's not enough to encourage you to march into this Ming masterpiece, consider grilled lamb chops in a coconut milk-curry sauce with pine nuts sprinkled over fresh greenery with a daikon salad.

THE OCEAN GRILL

SEAFOOD

MODERATE TO
EXPENSIVE

*6432
International
Drive, Orlando*
(407) 352-9993
*Lunch and
dinner daily*

There's prime rib, New York strips, Delmonicos and a half-dozen pastabilities on the menu along with barbecue ribs and chicken breast given what they call Italian and Hawaiian treatments, (one with marinara sauce, mozzarella and fettuccine, the other with a basting of teriyaki and a crown of grilled pineapple). But the real stars here are more loyal to the name, despite its distance from the saltwater. There's every kind of seafood selection from starters of conch fritters, fried calamari, blackened shrimp creole and New England clam chowder, to the main events built around fried catfish and shrimp; the San Francisco answer to bouillabaisse, seafood cioppino; English fish 'n' chips of baby cod; oven-baked salmon, with a dijon cream sauce, and grilled swordfish enlivened by fresh herbs and shallots pico de gallo on the side.

ITALIAN

MODERATE

*7653
International
Drive, Orlando
(407) 351-1082
Breakfast, lunch
and dinner daily*

THE OLIVE GARDEN ITALIAN RESTAURANT

Make a pilgrimage to this monument of American entrepreneurial genius and the talents of food giant General Mills' restaurant division, the same good folks who brought us Red Lobster (see page 83) and who are apparently going to succeed with their latest venture, China Coast (see page 48). This, the first of what is now a nationwide chain numbering more than 400 — with 50 new Olive Gardens harvesting dollars each year — opened on December 13, 1982.

The rest is history — the design, the use of umbrella tables, the development of takeout, the installation of a pasta maker near the entrance, and the perfecting of a menu that any kitchen can handle in volume with a minimum of complications or catastrophes. That means lasagna, veal and chicken given parmesan and marsala treatments, pastas in cream or tomato sauces mingled with scampi, snow crab, vegetables or meatballs, various combination plates and five dishes lower in calories, fat and cholesterol, such as minestrone, grilled chicken, orange roughy fillets and angel hair primavera. There's no end to the refills of soup and salad and the garlic-oil torpedo roll basket is never empty.

Unusual in this mega-chain, this Garden is a two-story operation and is open for breakfast, but perhaps that's part of a new prototype the bean-counters and marketeers are taking into consideration. In any case, this place provides a business school case study in how to succeed in the U.S. restaurant industry by cashing in on trends and creating family-pleasing food — unless that family happens to be Italian.

PASSAGE TO INDIA

There are two Indian restaurants with the same name on International Drive, and they are owned by a veteran of the Marriott Corporation, Uday Kadam. He put his experience to good use, creating well-dressed transports to the subcontinent, complete with sitar music softly playing in the background. You can seek his advice if you're in doubt about what to order — and how spicy — from the menu. We usually start with meat and vegetable samosas, hoping they are freshly made and not soggy, dipping our nan — the bread baked very quickly in the high heat tandoor — in the chilis and chutneys while we contemplate what kind of meat or vegetables to order with curry. Tandoori chicken is of course included along with the raita yogurt, OK with cucumber but essential with mint if anything with the suffix vindaloo is ordered.

INDIAN

MODERATE

5532 International Drive, Orlando (407) 351-3456 Lunch Monday through Friday Dinner daily

845 Sand Lake Road, Orlando (407) 856-8362 Dinner daily

MEDITERRANEAN

MODERATE

*The Marketplace
7600 Dr.
Phillips
Boulevard, suite
142, Orlando
(407) 345-1001
Lunch and
Dinner Daily*

PHOENICIAN RESTAURANT

Sah Tayn! Health to you! And to all those in
your tent who love *Labneh* and *Loubeigh Bil
Ziet,* pine for *Fa Sulye Plakisi,* and go bananas
over *Baba Ghanouj.* You'll find it all in this
Phoenician, the best Middle East restaurant in
Florida. Thanks to the experience, skill and
dedication of chef Amal, her husband Elias El
Rahi, son George, cousin Mounira Simaan
and a Moroccan chef named Yazza. Together
they do it all, from the *Baba Ghanouj* baked
eggplant pureed with garlic and lemon-
infused tahini, to the *Fa Sulye,* pinto beans
done the spicy Turkish way; from *Loubeigh
Bil,* cold broad beans with garlic, onions and
tomato, to the *Labneh,* which here and in
yogurt-loving Lebanon is fresh, homemade
and strained half a day until it reaches the
consistency of soft cheese — it's served with
mint and a splash of olive oil.

Our favorite feasting in this simply furnished oasis with white lattice dividers, a few
bunches of grapes dangling from the paddle
fans, a wall-filling mural of the old country
and a back counter for display and takeout,
includes all of the above plus an obligatory
bowl of *hummus,* chickpeas mashed and
merged with tahini, garlic and lemon juice,
garnished with sprigs of parsley and lightly
sprinkled with paprika and a drop or two of
olive oil. Then comes a bit of *falafel,* which
chef Amal does better than anyone this side of
the Mediterranean, carefully blending ground

fava beans and chick peas with different spices and then deep-frying the combination swiftly and christening it with tahini sauce and a bouquet of tomatoes, parsley and onions. It's followed by a bunch of grape leaves wrapped around ground beef, and the unique Phoenician sausages made by Elias, who had years of experience in the meat and poultry business before finding Florida as a new home.

And those are only the appetizers! We get down to the serious stuff with beef or lamb shish kebabs, the *Shawarma* dinner featuring marinated beef or chicken broiled vertically on a skewer basted with tahini sauce and served with pita bread for filling with the meat and layers of tomato and spiced onions. From chef Yazza's culinary traditions there's chicken, lamb and vegetable couscous to choose from — and it's as good as ever I had in Tangier or Fez. The Greeks inspired the moussaka, and, for those timid few in the group who can't ever be persuaded to try something new, there are shrimp scampi and filet mignon.

A proper finale to the feast — all in good time and without the slightest sense of rush — is Turkish coffee and one of the Phoenician desserts — best this side of Beirut. The well-known baklava or the less well-known *Katayef,* an Ashta cheese-filled shell covered with their own syrup and chopped pistachio nuts, or *Kalayef,* which is a *Katayef* filled with ground walnuts and deep-fried. *Sah Tayn!*

AMERICAN

INEXPENSIVE

*6362
International
Drive, Orlando
(407) 352-9343
Breakfast, lunch
and dinner daily*

*8510
International
Drive, Orlando
(407) 354-1477*

*14407
International
Drive
(407) 238-2526*

PONDEROSA RESTAURANT

Whoa partner! Come and get it! Here are enough vittles for Old Hoss and his ranch hands and all the rest of the crew of "Bonanza." Gigantic, humongous, awesome breakfast buffets and groaning tables noon and night overflow with more than 70 items — a super-sized salad bar that's also a place to pick up a few meatballs and chili, spaghetti or fettuccine, chicken wings and hot vegetables, plus desserts and fresh fruit. Your entrees include ribs and chicken, T-bones, rib eyes and sirloins, shrimp and lobster tails. These are high-profile, high-volume feeders where you can find plenty of freshness among the fried, and fill the family for the day — remembering the snack stuff you'll consume all day long.

JAPANESE

MODERATE

*8400
International
Drive, Orlando
(407) 345-0044
Dinner daily*

RAN-GETSU OF TOKYO, INC.

Simply put, this is the best Japanese restaurant in the country. A branch of a giant of the same name in Tokyo, it manages to retain a sense of intimacy and individual concern while operating on a high-volume (350 seats) basis. The S-shaped sushi bar, (easily the longest in Florida), provides catbird comfortable seating for watching the artistry of the sushi chef rolling the sticky rice, slicing the impeccably fresh tuna, eel, salmon, octopus, binding with seaweed wraps and assembling their original Florida roll filled with snow crab, avocado, cucumber, seaweed and sesame seeds. Stellar examples of Atarashii Ryori, Japanese nouvelle cuisine. The lower level tables are best for watching the ceremoniously garbed corps de kimono who shuffle dance to authentic Japanese music on the weekends and during traditional Japanese holidays. Depending on the weather, the performers go through those paces on an outdoor stage, strategically placed to afford maximum viewing. It's over a pond filled with the largest koi I've ever seen and flanked by typical Japanese garden plantings.

For light bites we remain parked at the sushi bar, but when we go the whole 90 yards, we sit at a table and start our evening in Japan with mussels steamed in sake, the Gyoza pork-stuffed dumplings with a hot mustard sauce, a tempura mix, or something really special: the Kubiyaki skewered gator meatballs or Orlando tofu steak, pan-fried and served with a special sauce.

For entrees we have trouble deciding among their many specialties. They include Ran-Getsu Bento, an array of authenticity beautifully arranged in a lacquer box; the dip-it-yourself Shabu-Shabu, given that name from the sound of the sirloin slices cooking in the *nabe,* the pot of broth before you; the Kaisen Yaki seafood grilled tableside, or the signature dish of the Tokyo Ran-Getsu for half a century, sukiyaki — remembering to pronounce it "skeeyaki".

Irrashaimase! Welcome to Ran-Getsu.

BARBECUE

INEXPENSIVE

*7629 Turkey
Lake Road,
Orlando
(407) 352-0080
Lunch and
dinner daily*

REAM & CO. BARBECUE CLUB

It's a club that's open to the public — the public that knows good 'cue when it passes between the lips, leaving a little ribbon of sauce oozing out of the corner of the mouth. The setting is the standard let's-look-like-back-country with corrugated steel sheeting, old timbers, all kinds of collectibles and just plain junk. But what the heck, it's really a couple of storefronts in an insignificant strip of small stores. The barbecue style here is Texas dry with beef brisket, ribs and pork prepared over hickory. If you don't know what Texas means you haven't been watching your Westerns and don't remember those wild chili cook-offs and barbecues made famous during the Johnson era in the White House. No namby-pamby North Carolina or Tennessee 'cue here, but strictly Rio Bravo beauts in a sauce that'll make a man out of you. But the real headliners are the baked beans drowned in a barbecue sauce, the rough-cut coleslaw and the smoked sweet potatoes. Place your order at the counter and have it delivered to your plain table where there's plenty of bottled fire plus a roll of paper towels for use after you're finished with all the finger lickin'.

RED LOBSTER

SEAFOOD

MODERATE

*5936
International
Drive, Orlando*
(407) 351-9313
*Lunch and
dinner daily*

*9892
International
Drive, Orlando*
(407) 345-0018

Unlike General Mills' Olive Garden (see page 76) and China Coast (see page 48), this mega-chain with more than 600 operations in the U.S. and Canada was not born on International Drive, but in Lakeland, Florida, 130 miles southwest of Orlando. From a simple little seafood server opened in 1968, the lobster has grown into a giant. It's a $1.6 billion business, the largest table-service dining network in North America. New ones are opening their doors at the rate of 50 a year and that includes cities as distant as Tokyo where there are 50 Red Lobsters — with Japanese menus of course, and, I suppose, sushi bars.

General Mills' seafood buyers search the world to find quality and quantity and you get the benefit, relying on the bulletin board for what's fresh that day, or sticking with such tried-and-true standbys as the platters with a variety of broiled, sauteed and fried seafood. It's a phenomenon!

SHOGUN JAPANESE STEAKHOUSE

JAPANESE

MODERATE

International Inn
6327 International Drive, Orlando
(407) 352-1607
Dinner daily

If you're not familiar with the Japanese Steakhouse routine — as in Benihana — here's a good place to spend a couple of hours. They opened in 1978, about the time James Clavell's *Shogun* novel was in its 27th printing. You'll sit shoulder-to-shoulder with friends or strangers, staring straight ahead to the blade-brandishing and chopstick-twirling Samurai, masquerading as chefs and sometimes stand-up comics. With the speed of light they slice the sirloin and de-tail the jumbo shrimp, displaying the dexterity of brain surgeons, and then swiftly saute the bean sprouts, onions and squash on the *teppan,* the smoking-sizzling grill. That drama before your very eyes is preceded by the corps de kimono delivering a small bowl of clear broth soup and simple salad. If you're seated with strangers, have no fear about conversation — someone is certain to own a Sony, a Toyota or have traveled to Tokyo.

SIAM ORCHID RESTAURANT

THAI/ASIAN

MODERATE

7576 Republic Drive, Orlando
(407) 351-0821
Lunch Monday through Friday
Dinner daily

Competing with Ming Court and Ran-Getsu (see pages 74 and 80) for title of most impressively evocative representation of the Orient, this temple of beautifully carved wood with marvelous statuary and authentic artifacts is a real treat for the eyes and the spirit. It encourages a sense of immersion in a foreign culture and its culinary traditions. If this is the first time you've Thai-ed one on, listen to the waitress as she offers advice and commentary on the menu. Some of the waitresses are native Thai, others American, but they're all dressed in colorful costumes to add to the atmosphere. We usually start with one of the soups and a few skewers of satay to make sure the back room is still blending a properly balanced peanut sauce, and then move on to mee grob, that crunchy stack of noodles, and an order of jumping shrimp with its sharp white onions and peppery zing. For the main attraction, we like most the whole red snapper coated with ginger and ever so crispy, or one of the curries calmed with coconut milk.

SIZZLER RESTAURANT

AMERICAN

INEXPENSIVE TO MODERATE

This chain takes the same basic approach as its prime competitor, Ponderosa, offering stuff-yourself-silly buffets morning, noon and night. It's not a poet-and-peasant overture to the steak, chicken and seafood entrees, but a peasant and peasant. Don't knock it; it's not overpriced, it's immaculately maintained, and there's plenty of fresh fruit and salad fixin's for those who don't want that much food. It's also a great place to take a family before or after all that walking in the parks or all that water-sliding at Wet 'n Wild.

9142 International Drive, Orlando (407) 351-5369 Breakfast, lunch and dinner daily

Delicatessens, Caterers and Takeout

The Marketplace
7600 Dr.
Phillips
Boulevard,
Orlando
(407) 352-2130

CHAMBERLIN'S NATURAL FOOD STORE

They have a fine inventory of foods for those who never want to get fat, and those who want vitamins, minerals and food supplements, or just a simple soup and sandwich from their self-serve counter, followed by frozen yogurt.

Goodings Plaza
8255
International
Drive, Orlando
(407) 352-4215

The Marketplace
7600 Dr.
Phillips
Boulevard,
Orlando
(407) 352-8851

GOODINGS

The ultimate American supermarket, a one-stop spacious and super-clean stunner that has everything, from one-hour photo processing, to flowers and souvenirs, fresh-baked goods and pharmaceutical supplies with a pharmacist on duty. The counters are bulging with lots of takeout, already packaged sandwiches and salads, and there's no end to the containers filled with freshly made pasta dishes and cold cuts for your own assembling — there's even ready-made Jell-O ready to go. On the premises are also little links of Kentucky Fried Chicken, Pizza Hut and Taco Bell for fast food freaks who want to eat before dropping from the shopping — there's an enclosed space by the sidewalk to do the eating. The Goodings by the Marketplace does not have those outlets or as much prepackaged fare, but they offer all the other eye-pleasing foodstuffs and necessities.

MERCADO MEDITERRANEAN VILLAGE

8445 International Drive, Orlando (407) 351-0692

In the main courtyard of the village — site of nightly entertainment — there are chairs, tables and benches for consuming your take-out fare from the adjacent village snackeries and mini-cafes. They offer everything from wok 'n' roll to deli sandwiches and South of the Border stuff, burgers and hot dogs to Greek gyros and South American empanadas, Cajun chicken to Italian gelato and American ice cream, and at Sweet Sensations, fresh-baked beauties and frozen yogurt.

SHOPPING

WHEN IT COMES TO SHOPPING, THE NAME OF I-Drive could be changed to Buy Drive, Discount Drive, Bargain Boulevard. The stores with signs shouting savings are everywhere, dominating strip malls, large and small. Come out of a restaurant and walk a few feet to find Shell City, diamonds, luggage and shoes, casual clothing, golf and tennis gear, a zillion T-shirts and electronic everything. When the theme park going gets tough, the tough go shopping — next door to their breakfast buffet or across the street from their hotel. There's an outlet for each day of the year — 465 of them, or maybe it's 565! Many are gathered together — for those who really can shop till they drop — in a monstrous mallplex of cut-rate merchandise on the northern end of Discount Drive at Belz Factory Outlet World.

BELZ FACTORY OUTLET WORLD

This shopper's dream has more than 700,000 square feet of bargains in two giant malls and four annexes. Owned by a German limited

partnership investment group, Belz boasts
it's the second-largest tourist attraction in
Florida with some 12 million visitors a year.
With about 180 stores, it is certainly the
largest such center to be found anywhere in
Florida, the nation and maybe the world. It
even has a carousel for the kids — in Mall 2
near the food court — and there's plenty of
free parking.

Shoppers who know comparative costs are
obviously the best prepared to buy here. They
charge into seek-and-buy missions, purchasing
name-brand merchandise from kitchen cutlery,
linens, dishes, pots, pans and all kinds of
housewares to jewelry, linens and accessories,
lingerie, health and beauty aids, cameras,
videos, VCRs and other electronic gear; from
accessories, souvenirs, gift items and toys to
books, records, tapes and enough shoes to out-
fit an army.

Among the clothing designers represented
here are Jordache and Geoffrey Beene, Adolfo
and Van Heusen, Oshkosh B'Gosh, Jonathan
Logan, Burlington, London Fog and Cape Isle
Knitters, Sergio Tacchini, Danskin, Calvin
Klein, Bugle Boy, Polly Flinders and Gitano.

5401 West Oak Ridge Road (northern end of
International Drive), Orlando
(407) 352-9600

DANSK FACTORY OUTLET

Dansk has its own free-standing shop on the Drive, and it was one of the first to pioneer the concept of bargain-shopping in the area. We used to stop by here to save money in the early 1970s when there was very little traffic on the Drive and very few places to eat. Beautiful teak bowls and boxes, table accessories, china, glassware and flatware and select plastic kitchenware for the home and office all come from Dansk Design.

7000 International Drive, Orlando
(407) 351-2425

MERCADO MEDITERRANEAN VILLAGE

There are more than 60 shops in the Village, considerably more upscale in location and inventory than those found in the rack-to-the-back discount outlets. The shops are more intimate than imposing and the range of merchandise international with Irish, Mexican, African and Asian imports, paintings and sculptures, licensed World Cup soccer (coming to Orlando in '94) clothing and equipment, plus comparable souvenirs from professional American teams, Western and tropical wear, wind chimes and a unique bookstore where the volumes are color coded, hammocks, collector dolls and bears and of course, the Disney and Universal Studios stuff.

8445 International Drive, Orlando
(407) 345-9337

Shells

SEA SHELL LADY
7551 Canada Avenue, Orlando
(407) 363-9312

SHELL WORLD INTERNATIONAL
6464 International Drive, Orlando
(407) 351-0900
(407) 352-8937

8540 International Drive, Orlando
(407) 354-5755

CONVENIENCES

Barber and Beauty Shops

ABOUT HAIR

This salon is open seven days a week and walk-ins are welcome. They carry Sebastian products and the staff is proficient in creating the right style for every member of the family.

4610 Kirkman Road, Orlando
(407) 290-0707

CAVALLO HAIR DESIGNERS

A beautiful, totally mod place for obtaining that beautiful, mod hairstyle. This is a full-service unisex salon offering cuts, colors, perms, waxing and manicures. They also have a patented spiral perming service.

The Marketplace
7600 Dr. Phillips Boulevard, Orlando
(407) 351-3647

DUE MONDI II

This full-service salon has stylists who have studied in various parts of the globe from Italy and Israel to Puerto Rico. But most of the stylists are from Europe.

5660 International Drive, Orlando
(407) 352-3555

THE HAIR CUTTERY

This is a chain of salons noted for being great, inexpensive places to keep the family looking good with the latest hairstyles.

Mercado Village North
8255 International Drive, suite 1790, Orlando
(407) 351-8628

HAIR POWER SALON & SPA

You can really pamper yourself on your vacation in this full-service salon and spa with massages and facials, or even take aerobics classes to shape up and go home looking like a million.

1650 Sand Lake Road, Orlando
(407) 851-4101

HAIR STUDIO LIMITED

Award-winning stylists perform wonders with cuts, coloring and perms, and technicians do their number with nail treatments, waxing and facials. This full-service unisex salon caters to all ages.

4890 South Kirkman Road, Orlando
(407) 299-8947

STRICTLY NAILS

This is the place for the latest technology in nail care — manicures, extensions, buildups. That's all they do.

4900 S. Kirkman Road, Orlando
(407) 290-9561

TOTAL MAN

These professional technicians specialize in total cosmetology services created just for men.

4900-B South Kirkman Road, Orlando
(407) 292-1544

TOUCH OF CLASS BY MARIA LUCHI

All the stylists in this salon are trained in Europe and are artistically creative. When it comes to custom styling a cut just for you they do a wonderful job. They are equally well-schooled in coloring, perming and all areas of cosmetology.

5905 International Drive, Orlando
(407) 352-4209

Business Needs

APEX OFFICE PRODUCTS, INC.

2484 Sand Lake Road, Orlando
(407) 856-4273

COURIER COMPANIES

7575 Dr. Phillips Boulevard, Orlando
(407) 345-1647

DEE JAY PRINTING & DESIGN

Central Park
2440 Sand Lake Road, Orlando
(407) 851-8544

KAREPAK USA

4959 Sand Lake Road, Orlando
(407) 352-5675

KENNEDY PRINTERS INC.

54 South Kirkman Road, Orlando
(407) 294-7920

MAILBOXES ETC.

4630 South Kirkman Road, Orlando
(407) 578-6322

MINUTEMAN PRESS

1931 Sand Lake Road, Orlando
(407) 826-0805

MR. POSTMAN

The one-stop place for office supplies, mailing
and shipping services, fax and copy services.

Goodings Plaza
Mercado Mediterranean Village
8445 International Drive, suite 111, Orlando
(407) 352-3540

PACKAGING STORE

"The Shipper Who Does the Packing Too!" is their slogan. Whether it's domestic or foreign, they can handle the job — from small jobs like a shopping spree for souvenirs and gifts, to fragile china and antiques, to the large task of shipping furniture and automobiles. And they have a pickup service.

Williamsburg Downs Shopping Center
5334 Central Florida Parkway (at International Drive), Orlando
(407) 238-1000

TURKEY LAKE PRESS

They have bindery services, laminating, color copies, resume, stationery, color paper, laid, stone and linen book binding, typesetting and fax services.

4900-A South Kirkman Road, Orlando
(407) 293-4800

Child Care

ALL ABOUT KIDS

All babysitters are certified in CPR, wear photo I.D.s and Kelly green golf shirts, are insured, bonded and licensed. They come to your hotel, condo, or home, accompanying the family to keep an eye on the little ones, or giving you a complete break by taking the kids sightseeing or to the parks. There is a small transportation fee. They also rent strollers, cribs and car seats.

Osceola County: (407) 933-4424
Toll-free: 1-800-728-6506

Dry Cleaners and Laundromats

CONTEMPORARY CLEANERS

4882 Kirkman Road, Orlando
(407) 295-1414

JAZM CLEANERS INC.

811 Sand Lake Road, Orlando
(407) 240-3569

OAK RIDGE LAUNDROMAT

2396 West Oak Ridge Road, Orlando
(407) 855-9274

Photography Supplies and Processing

There are many places up and down International Drive where you can buy photographic equipment and get your vacation photos processed in a flash. In the discount outlets in the area there is at least one in each strip of shops.

KOLOR PHOTO & CAMERA

The Marketplace
7600 Dr. Phillips Boulevard, suite 98, Orlando
(407) 352-6096

RENT-A-CAM, INC.

You can rent a great little hand-held, light-weight video camera. They are so easy to use, you're sure to capture the right scene, and remember the sounds of joy from the fun you had on your vacation. You could get a shot you would like to turn into a still picture.

604 International Drive, Orlando
(407) 345-9460

Shoe Repair

McCRORY 5 & 10

Same-day service shoe repairs.

Turkey Lake Village
4780 South Kirkman Road, Orlando
(305) 293-6402

Taxi and Limousine Service

AIRPORT SHUTTLE SERVICE ORLANDO

(407) 657-1900

AIR TRANSPORT CO.

Ride in the comfort of a Lincoln Town Car on your way to or from the airport.

(407) 382-0404

ALTAMONTE CAB CO.

You can plan your trip to the minute with prearranged pickup at the airport and delivery to your hotel.

(407) 657-1331

DESIGNATED DRIVER SERVICE, INC.

At an inexpensive rate, your group can have a safe outing with a licensed chauffeur in the driver's seat who knows the area attractions.

(407) 671-9998

ELITE CENTRAL FLORIDA LIMOUSINES

Luxury limousines with VCRs, CD players and color TVs.

(407) 695-7554

FIRST CLASS LIMOUSINE SERVICE

(407) 578-0022

MEARS TRANSPORTATION GROUP, INC.

Included in this group are City Cab (407-422-5151), Yellow Cab (407-699-9999), both in business since 1939; and Luxury Limousine Service (407-843-5553, toll-free: 1-800-759-5219). They're big enough and have been in business long enough to be trusted to get you there.

324 West Gore Street, Orlando
(407) 422-5151

MAJOR ATTRACTIONS

FUN 'N WHEELS

In addition to the racetrack, there are bump
boats, a water slide ride, a Ferris wheel, an
arcade and a souvenir shop.

International Drive and Sand Lake Road, Orlando
(407) 351-5651

MALIBU GRAND PRIX

There are formula-style race cars, as well as
batting cages so it's not the place to take the
littlest ones. But they might like the video
games and the mini-miniature golf.

5863 American Way (International Drive), Orlando
(407) 351-7093

MYSTERY FUN HOUSE

This is not an all-day affair, or even an hour-
long affair, and that might add to the fun of
making your way through a maze, laughing at
the wall of mirrors, dodging the lasers and…
Well, it's supposed to be a mystery so you and
your little ones can discover it for yourselves.

5767 Major Boulevard, Orlando
(407) 351-3355

SEA WORLD

This largest of all marine parks in the world, all 135 acres of it, is owned by beer giant Anheuser-Busch, which owns other Sea Worlds in California, Ohio and Texas as well as Busch Gardens and Adventure Island in Tampa, and Cypress Gardens (famous for its fabulous water-skiers) in nearby Winter Haven. If you want to do this park well, you'll need the better part of a day. The best approach is to check the handout map you're given at the entrance and determine the times of the various shows, especially the featured attractions and especially Shamu, the 8,000-pound killer whale who performs in an $18 million stadium. You'll also want to see the Whale and Dolphin Show, experience the Bermuda Triangle, and walk through the fascinating Terrors of the Deep tunnel with the sharks swimming all about you — every which way but loose! There are penguins to marvel at, seals and sea lions, walrus and sea otters performing and an exhibit, the newest, titled "Manatees: The Last Generation?" It's devoted to Florida's gentle and slow-moving giants — they can reach a weight of 3,000 pounds — whose future is seriously threatened by recreational boating and loss of habitat.

7007 Sea World Drive, Orlando
(407) 351-3600

UNIVERSAL STUDIOS FLORIDA

There's no larger studio production lot outside of Hollywood, and be sure to study the layout on the map you'll be given at the entrance. Opened in 1990 at a cost of $600 million, its 444 acres are filled with enough fascination to keep the family fully occupied for at least a day — and then you'll still miss some of the attractions. There are more than 50 of them, including the best of all the rides in any of the parks, Back to the Future. The encounters with King Kong, E.T., Ghostbusters, Earthquake and Rocky and Bullwinkle are also very definitely worth your time. Alfred Hitchcock, Angela Lansbury (*Murder She Wrote*) and Lucille Ball fans will love their space on the lot and, for those who always wanted to be in one of those monster movies, there's the Gory, Gruesome and Grotesque Horror Make-up Show. Future animators will learn something from The Funtastic World of Hanna-Barbera. And as you move from one ride, store, restaurant and show to another you'll be walking through midtown Manhattan, Hollywood Boulevard and a wonderful series of television and movie sets.

For those who think they might want a career on screen or tube there's the Nickelodeon Studios where you can stop by the "Gak Meister's kitchen," get "slimed" and participate in a game show, and on a more serious note, the studios where you can get into the

action and make your own screen debut.
Here's how one enthusiast described the expe-
rience during our most recent visit to
Universal:

"I loved the studio where you could make
your own audio recording, sing with the
band so to speak (canned music) and the
room for shooting your own music video.
That was great fun. But the most excite-
ment was discovering I could make my
own mini-movie with big-name stars,
sound effects, special effects backdrops.
What a feeling to be outfitted in my own
spacesuit and be led through the steps of
shooting scenes for a show — cue cards on
the walls, marked spots on the floor for perfect positioning. Everything was so
well-organized and easy. They made it so
much fun to walk through the lines and
watch a monitor to see how the scene was
actually being filmed. Then to go to the
lobby and watch the finished product on a
television set — what a high! Especially for
a Trekkie. Captain Kirk and Mr. Spock,
Scotty and Uhura, Chekov and Dr.
"Bones" McCoy, and real Klingons were all
there. Not really; they were superimposed.
But who has to know?"

1000 Universal Studios Plaza, Orlando
(407) 363-8000

WET 'N WILD

This 25-acre water park complete with a six-story, four-passenger ride called Bubba Tub, a 76-foot, free-fall water slide called Bomb Bay, and the Robo-Surfer, a mechanical surfboard, is the nation's most attended park of its kind. The fun doesn't stop with water sports activities. They also have live bands playing daily, trivia and pizza- and sub-eating contests and beach games such as tug of war.

6200 International Drive, Orlando
(407) 351-1800
Toll-free: 1-800-992-WILD (9453)

ENTERTAINMENT

Bookstores

BOOK WAREHOUSE

Belz Factory Outlet World, Annex 1, Orlando
(407) 345-1110
(407) 345-0223

BOOKLAND BOOK OUTLET

Belz Factory Outlet World, Mall 1, Orlando
(407) 351-6754

NOVEL IDEAS-AN ADVENTURE IN BOOKS INC.

A must stop for bookworms of all ages. They
have a great program for kids through the teen
years, a comics section for the avid collector
and the latest (not just the critics choice) in
paperbacks and hardcovers.

Mercado Mediterranean Village
8445 South International Drive, suite 114, Orlando
(407) 363-2850

Bowling

WORLD BOWLING CENTER
Dowdy Pavilion, 7540 Canada Avenue, Orlando
(407) 352-2695

Dinner Shows

EXPENSIVE

*7007 Sea World
Drive, Orlando
(407) 363-2559
Dinner daily*

ALOHA! POLYNESIAN LUAU

Wonderful, colorful South Pacific theme
complete with choreographed hula dancers,
sword whirlers and fire twirlers. It's an exciting display of song and dance from the
Islands with an enjoyable dinner featuring the
best food to be found in any of the dinner
shows anywhere. You kick off with one of
those bound-to-bring-giggles-to-the-kids pu
pu platters with lots of fruit, a salad with
coconut-sesame dressing, entrees of dolphin,
smoked pork, sweet and sour chicken with
appropriate Polynesian vegetables and white
rice, followed by some excellent cheesecake.
But there are no bottomless bottles of bever-
ages — after the welcoming drink, you're on
your own.

ASIAN ADVENTURE

A dazzling performance by unbelievably agile acrobats, jugglers, magicians and practitioners of martial arts. Go along with them on a grand tour of China, Hong Kong, Japan and Thailand, and enjoy the music and the five-course meal. It includes unlimited beer, wine, soda, and consists of egg drop soup, an egg roll, Oriental beef and chicken with vegetables, fried rice, dessert and, for finishers, what else but a fortune cookie?

EXPENSIVE

International Station
5225 International Drive, Orlando
(407) 351-5655
Dinner daily

HILARITIES COMEDY THEATRE

You can get a belly laugh and a bellyful in this theater that features big-name comedy acts seen on HBO, the *Comedy Corner* and *The Tonight Show*. Ask to be set up with a dinner package.

MODERATE

5251 International Drive, Orlando
(407) 363-1920
Shows Tuesday through Saturday

KING HENRY'S FEAST

This is the Dean of the Dinner Shows, performed in a 14,000-square-foot fortified English manor house complete with moat out front and tower up top. It's a 500-seat, $3.5 million eye-popper with a dozen make-believe British characters, including Henry VIII of course. It's another extravaganza brought to us by Pleasurama of London, the same folks responsible for Mardi Gras (see page 117) and Caruso's Palace (see page 43).

EXPENSIVE

8984 International Drive, Orlando
For reservations, call Orlando Entertains:
(407) 351-5151
Dinner daily

This immersion into medieval times with lots of audience participation commences with a welcoming cup of mead, that medieval brew that encouraged contemporaries to hurry into the Renaissance, and continues with a five-course banquet served family-style — soup, salad, roast chicken and ribs, veggies and pie a la mode, plus the usual all-you-can-drink beer (not mead, thank heavens!), wine and sodas — but in tankards. The entertainment includes a diverse group of performers: a magician, an aerialist, dueling knights, a sword swallower and a court jester who aids Henry in his search for a seventh wife.

MARDI GRAS

EXPENSIVE

Mercado Mediterranean Village

8445 International Drive, Orlando

For reservations, call Orlando Entertains: (407) 351-5151

Dinner daily

You won't have to wait until Easter to enjoy the fun and high jinks of a Mardi Gras extravaganza. The entertainers include Dixielanders and dancers, singers and acrobats, jugglers and comedians who give their all in a two-hour high-energy performance, while you work through a four-course dinner with all-you-can-drink beer, wine and Coca-Cola. The Caesar salad, chicken breast, dressing and Key lime pie are nothing to write New Orleans about, but it's acceptable — as long as the performance is of such high caliber.

SLEUTHS MYSTERY DINNER THEATER

EXPENSIVE

Republic Square 7508 Republic Drive (at the northern end of International Drive), Orlando (407) 363-1985

Dinner daily

Here's the place to play Sherlock or Miss Marple as you enter into the mystery and mingle with the quartet of actors, being careful to watch for clues as you work through a pretty good meal built around hot and cold hors d'oeuvres, honey-glazed Cornish hen with herb stuffing, rice pilaf and mixed vegetables, preceded by a mixed green salad and followed by a mystery dessert. It's accompanied by unlimited beer, wine and soft drinks.

Golf

CONGO RIVER GOLF & EXPLORATION COMPANY

Explore the wilds of the Congo on two 18-hole miniature courses.

6312 International Drive, Orlando
(407) 352-0042

INTERNATIONAL GOLF CLUB

There are terrific golf courses all over the Orlando area, and one of the best is right on International Drive, at the southern stretches of the grand boulevard. The 18-hole par 72 was designed by Joe Lee, one of the greats in golf course design and layout. Lee is responsible for the courses at Walt Disney World, Miami Beach's Doral Country Club with its infamous Blue Monster, La Costa in California, as well as links scattered around the Caribbean and Central America. What Lee did here was give golfers a challenge, "but a fair one." You can discuss whether or not it's fair in the clubhouse locker rooms and lounge. Then you can find a better putter in the fully stocked pro shop and practice with it on the putting green, saving your big muscle activity for the lighted practice range.

6351 International Golf Club Road, Orlando
(407) 239-6909

PIRATE'S COVE

8601 International Drive, Orlando
(407) 352-7378

Miniature golf with 18 holes.

Ice Skating

ROCK ON ICE!

Rock on this Olympic-sized, regulation sur-
face rink where you can take lessons to help
you look like a contender or learn to play
hockey with the best. Bring some warm clothing to wear; it's a great way to cool off on a
hot day, but it does get cold.

Dowdy Pavilion
7500 Canada Avenue, Orlando
(407) 363-RINK (7465)

Lounges and Nightclubs

BACKSTAGE AT THE CLARION

International Drive is not known for its nightlife, although there are lounges with dance floors and live entertainment; but there are some 80 magnets off the Drive, places like Disney World's Pleasure Island [(407) 934-7781], downtown Orlando's Church Street Station complex [(407) 422-2434] or its neighboring rock 'n' roll piano bar, the Howl at the Moon Saloon [(407) 841-4695], currently the No. 1 draw with its dueling pianos and long lines waiting for a chance to jam with the mobs.

The closest in spirit to that kind of popularity on the Drive is the Backstage Lounge, cleverly designed to resemble behind the scenes of a movie set with lots of state-of-the-art light and sound systems. There are giant television screens showing MTV headliners in between sets of live entertainment, which ranges from the house band SOUNDTRAX, named Florida Band of the Year in 1992, to sing-along Karaoke, disco revivals and live taping of *The Singles Game* TV show. There are all kinds of drink promotions — free drinks for the ladies, bargain-priced margaritas, discounted beer and wine. If you're looking for a high-decibel, lively spot with gyrating dancers and hot bods, this is the place.

Clarion Plaza, 9700 International Drive, Orlando (407) 352-9700; (407) 354-1719

FAT TUESDAY

Where else would a Fat Tuesday be but close to Mardi Gras? — in this case not New Orleans on one particular pre-Lenten night, but on International Drive close by the supper club of the same name. It's Fat Tuesday each and every night of the year, but during most months of the year Tuesdays do get some special attention — like drink specials all night long. Other nights there might be a dollar off the large (and we do mean large) daiquiri of the week, with names such as 190 Octane, White Russian, Magic Potion and Killer Bees. Monday nights mean crawfish boil when management puts out 400 pounds of those little devils, along with all the fixins' for an all-you-can-eat free buffet during happy hour. There's live entertainment, an outdoor patio dance floor and what they declare to be the "World's Largest Selection of Frozen Drinks" — with names to remember — Jungle Juice, Bahama Mama, Banana Banshee, Triple Bypass, Lynchburg Lemonade, Tropical Itch and Purple Passion.

Mercado Mediterranean Village
8445 International Drive, Orlando
(407) 351-5311

Movies

MOVIES AT REPUBLIC SQUARE
7488 Republic Drive, Orlando
(407) 352-2601

SAND LAKE 7 CINEMAS
835 Sand Lake Road, Orlando
(407) 855-6380

Museums

ORLANDO TOY TRAIN MUSEUM
If you're a train buff this is the place for you. This is the largest indoor G-gauge toy train layout in the country, 14,000 square feet of it, with model engines and cars from the early years of the century to the most modern exemplars, a dozen of them puffing and gliding along simultaneously in a wonderful multi-media presentation. The shop out front has all kinds of trains and sets for you to start your own collection. And off in a corner is a small display of some of the great old American Flyers by a train collector, repairer and replacer who will be glad to discuss your particular needs. When you finish touring the shop and museum, take a ride on the full-size

narrow gauge carriages pulled around the
complex by an authentic steam engine, chug-
ging past such odd train station mates as the
Asian Adventure (see page 115) and a discount Lenox store.

5253 International Drive, Orlando
(407) 363-9002

RIPLEY'S BELIEVE IT OR NOT!

The first time I walked past this built-on-the-
cant, eye-catching structure I was so
fascinated looking at it that I lost my footing
on the level pavement. Inside is the kind of
stuff that the imaginative Robert Ripley
unearthed — sometimes literally — in his
world travels. Oddities from everywhere, grue-
some and gory at times, historic at others —
such as the large section of the infamous
Berlin Wall. See for yourself what this newest
of the several Believe It or Not! displays in
this country has to intrigue and amaze.

8201 International Drive, Orlando
(407) 872-3081

Swimming

YMCA AQUATIC CLUB

Located behind the Radisson Hotel, this club features a 50-meter pool for competition, a 25-yard training pool and a diving well. Classes are held on various water sports such as diving, water polo, synchronized and other swimming lessons, and lifeguard certification. You don't have to be a YMCA member to use this aquatic complex, but there are privileges you can take advantage of if you are. And there is a complete health club with free weights, aerobics and circuit training.

8422 International Drive, Orlando
(407) 363-1911

Index

About the Author

For more than a quarter-century Robert Tolf
has been traveling the state of Florida by foot,
car, train, boat and plane. A prolific writer
with more than 30 books to his credit, he is
the restaurant critic and featured travel colum-
nist for the Fort Lauderdale *Sun-Sentinel* and
restaurant editor of *Florida Trend* magazine.